Becoming Mister Ross
A Story of Growth, Connection, and Healing
Mister Ross

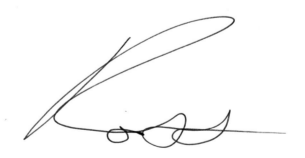

Kim,

Thank you for encouraging me + letting me know I'm a writer + poet,

Mister Ross Creations

Library of Congress Control Number: 2024910074

Copyright © 2024 by Mister Ross

All rights reserved.

No portion of this book may be reproduced in any form without written permission from the publisher or author, except as permitted by U.S. copyright law.

Cover design by Market Share Consulting

Photograph of author by Market Share Consulting

Contents

Dedication	1
Introduction	2
1. Setting the Stage	4
2. Childhood	8
3. High School	20
4. Home Away From Home Undergrad	30
5. My Near-Death Experience	41
6. Grad School My True College Experience	48
7. My First Counseling Experiences	53
8. Humble Beginnings Counseling (HBC)	57
9. Moving Forward & Faith Intentional Treatment Counseling (ITC)	69
10. Drama, Politics, and Management Intentional Treatment Counseling (ITC)	90
11. Courageous Counseling Practice (CCP)	100
12. The New Business & OCD Strikes Back	112
13. Mister Ross Counseling LLC	125

14. Conclusion	141
Epilogue	144
Acknowledgements	145
About the author	148
Enjoy Mister Ross' writing?	149

For my younger selves,
We made it.

Introduction

I was in a counseling session with Bill, my sage, white-haired counselor who held a striking resemblance to Ted Danson. I was explaining a struggle I had, one that in most people's eyes wasn't much of a problem at all. When I had finished, my counselor said to me, "Sometimes it's just not easy being Ross." We both laughed. This became an inside joke in therapy when we both knew I was making my problems bigger than they were. I found it fitting that this joke between counselor and client translated to the working title of my first book.

In my early career as a counselor, I learned to stand up for myself, depend more on God, and find my identity. This is my coming-of-age story. In numerous ways, this might be your story too. Overall, I recognize how God has worked through me in many ways, giving me more than I deserve and allowing me to use my journey, including the struggles and difficult times, to help others.

I'm not quite sure what inspired me to write this book, but it became about helping others, and, in doing that, it is deeply personal. At times it was painful to recall memories I'd rather forget. The idea of a stranger reading about some of the worst times in my life was scary and left me feeling vulnerable. I procrastinated often, not writing for weeks or months at a time. Sometimes I'd receive confirmation from those around me — I'm sure through divine intervention — to write more.

God has undoubtedly driven the most important aspects of my life. He profoundly influenced my path toward becoming a counselor and a more fulfilled, whole person. Had I turned away from my faith, therapy, or incredible support system, I would have been stuck, lost, and miserable. My once obsessive state of mind would have engulfed my sanity and happiness. I would not be anyone's counselor.

This book flows among my personal life, faith encounters, and clinical experiences as a mental health counselor from my first six years in the field. Along the way, I share relevant counseling insights. When speaking about therapy, I may use the words therapy and counseling interchangeably. Therapy and therapist are umbrella terms. My academic training and licensure is in counseling, so I lean toward using the words "counseling" and "counselor" over their related counterparts.

This book is written for the one, analogous to how God leaves the ninety-nine sheep to find the one lost member of the flock. There is much to gain on the journey of personal growth. Showing up, such as through reading a book like this, creates the opportunity for optimism, insight, and change for oneself. Connection to another is the impetus for change.

May this book find its way to a therapist, client, student, or concerned loved one who needs to hear my story and may experience the divine intervention that this book could hopefully offer. Healing and recovery in mental health is possible. Vulnerability is more than acceptable — it is strong and courageous. Achieving important goals, as one of my counselors said, is "doable." Helping others is always valuable. And you are worthy. I hope this book helps you believe all of this.

This story became one of testimony. I felt a conviction to share how my experiences as a counselor, client, and person weaved together to *Becoming Mister Ross*.

Chapter One
Setting the Stage

Insight: Pain

In the field of counseling, I have learned the traumas people go through, the struggles they endure, and the lifestyles they maintain. Addiction, broken relationships, abuse, stress, panic attacks, and abrupt changes and tragedies became the norm. Disconnection from God, family, friends, society, themselves, and reality were expected. I often have been the one to tell clients that they aren't crazy, despite the unhealthy people and bizarre circumstances surrounding them. No series or movie could capture some of the stories I've been told.

I've found that therapy is a special way to heal from my pain. I've used it from the client's chair to learn more about my journey — where my blindspots are, where I've grown, and where I might need to put more focus in my life. Meanwhile, from the counselor's chair, I sometimes heard clients share issues that touched on some of my own. In that moment, I might have felt a revelation, realizing that I went through a similar situation myself that cosmically prepared me to help them — and me — learn.

I'd wonder in awe at God's timing and beam in gratitude.

Oftentimes, suffering seems meaningless. Our hurt overtakes us, leading to more suffering as we process what occurred and build resentments toward ourselves and others. When we can help another with what pained us is when we can find purpose in the suffering. Likewise, when others help us in our suffering, this creates a bond — even if just for a moment — and, therefore, a purpose. While we *still* may wish the pain never occurred, we can find some consolation.

Therapy by its very nature then is filled with bittersweet, meaningful purpose.

Insight: Vulnerability

As a counselor, I hope my clients see me as a person. I want to help as I was helped. In this way, I'm as much a peer as a professional listener. I don't know if my clients realize much of the skills, feedback, and analogies I use are "hand-me-downs" from my own work. Some weeks I'm going through the same life lessons as my clients. Fortunately I might be enough steps ahead in my own life to help them with theirs.

I'm not just a professional with a bunch of degrees and letters after my name. I'm not simply a small-business owner or an overly sensitive, lost young male in a predominantly female-driven field. I'm not a shell of a person bound so closely by ethics and theory that I'm incapable of offering a genuine response.

I, too, have a story.

Letting people see you in the same manner they let you see them takes vulnerability. There's an element of risk here that the client won't like what you have to say or, worse, might not like you. That's the fear behind the imposter syndrome that says, "I'm not enough as a therapist," with the core fear or pain point being, "I'm not enough."

We don't like imposter syndrome or vulnerability walking in on us while we're playing the great and powerful Oz. But when the curtain gets pulled back, there we are, as we are. Why hide it and make the client have to travel the yellow brick road to find us? Aren't we supposed to meet them where they are and offer them what they need there?

Ultimately, my main concern in writing this book boiled down to, "Will people like me?" And at its core, "Am I enough?"

I consider the impressions left by some of my heroes. Fred Rogers, warmly remembered as Mister Rogers, carried an aura of kindness and caring wherever he went. His authenticity was undeniable, especially with children. Meanwhile, expertise in the fields of child development, media, and music helped him develop one of America's finest children's television shows, *Mister Rogers' Neighborhood*. Bob Ross, the famous television host and painter, also brought a calming nature balanced with a playfulness to both his art and his audience. He unapologetically shared his passions and enthusiasm. Additionally, Jim Henson brought a creativity and whimsical nature. Most famously, his personality extended to the characters of Kermit the Frog and Ernie from *Sesame Street*.

I wondered whether my fellow therapists would recommend this book to their clients, and whether those clients would find solace in seeing the transparent image of a real-life therapist. Yet, on the other side of creativity lay anxiety. Perhaps all the bookstores would do was hide a copy among the plethora of self-help books, or my donated copies would go unread at the local library.

Part of me felt it would be unimportant to give much priority to the praise or criticism I might receive. Yet, I'm human, seemingly hard-wired to gauge others' perceptions, seek validation, and connect with others.

What vulnerability offers is stronger bonds and more loving relationships. Asking others what you need or want takes vulnerability. Being able to listen to criticism and respond authentically takes vulnerability. Sharing how you actually are takes vulnerability.

Having written this book, I've chosen a different path by laying my story out there.

Insight: Being Genuine

This insight is for my fellow therapists and helpers. Being genuine is the most important skill of a successful therapist. Clients and people in general appreciate when they see us as simply us, not an "expert" in their midst. The more authentic you are, the more meaningful and effective your sessions will be. People will trust that you're with them from a place of understanding rather than a place of power or status. Therapists need to be able to laugh and cry with their clients and let their clients be themselves, all in a way consistent with the person who walks out the door when the session ends.

Following arbitrary standards may interfere with being genuine. As a "perfectionist in recovery," I've learned to lower expectations of myself, enjoy activities more, and become less rigid. Clinically, I've become more open-minded and less tied to certain outcomes or expectations of how counseling "should" be. I feel much more at ease with genuinely delivering what I have to say and presenting myself to my clients.

Consider the ways that make you *you*. Maybe you stare off into space as you ponder a response. Perhaps you talk slowly. You might be very direct with those around you. Your humor might have appropriate timing and perspective. You might use silence better than any of your peers. Maybe you allow your client to know how you feel in the moment with them, even when it might be easier to leave on the professional hat. Being genuine requires a little vulnerability to shine through.

Chapter Two
Childhood

Sweet Baby Ross

My parents say I was a colicky, difficult baby who had trouble falling asleep, which became a persistent issue throughout my life. At 30 days old, I had a spinal tap and was held to the table by doctors in white coats. I wondered if my irritability in crowded places was linked to this early trauma.

My mom tells a story about my first steps. Concerned that I hadn't started walking yet, she brought up her worries with my sage pediatrician.

"He can crawl?" the pediatrician asked.

"Yes," my mother replied.

"But he can't walk yet?"

"No."

"Well, let's see," he said, picking me up and placing me on the cold, ceramic tiles of the office. Immediately, I ran across the floor from the doctor to my mom. I didn't walk with those first steps — I ran.

But I wonder if those steps happened out of love for someone comfortable (my mother) or rather fear, as I ran away from the unfamiliar (the doctor). Running toward what I love or running away from what I fear has felt like a recurrent theme in my life.

Bye, Mom!: Starting School

I was a sociable child who loved school. My mom would laugh as she shared stories about how I had to be the first one to arrive for preschool to sit in the same seat. While I vaguely remember this routine, I do remember the anxiety I felt if I didn't sit in "my" spot.

I also hated having paint on my fingers thanks to two events, one of which occurred when a local clown painted designs on my peers' faces but I opted for a Power Ranger on my hand. On another occasion, my kindergarten classmates and I made a T-shirt with handprints for our teacher who was on leave. The idea of getting paint on my hands was excruciating, and my mother volunteered the next day to convince me to participate. I was brave in adding my handprints to the shirt and then awkwardly rushed to the sink with my outstretched hands.

Most people would have considered me a happy child. And despite my early neuroses, I enjoyed school — but that love would be short-lived.

In the Basement of a Church

Going to Catholic school from kindergarten through grade twelve was a blessing and a struggle. The structure of Catholic schools typically differs significantly from public schools. Catholic schools are more regimented, with stricter rules ranging from classroom etiquette to uniforms. The uniforms typically consisted of turtlenecks or polos with the school's name embroidered on them, or a button-down shirt with a tie and blue sport coat; boys wore slacks, and girls wore skirts. Teachers earned less than their public school counterparts, which meant, at times, that they had a more intrinsic reason to be there.

Religion and theology classes were part of the curriculum, which lacked content such as specialized education, music, art, home economics, technology, and sex education. We casually said prayers at the beginning of class, and crosses hung by every doorway. On one of the first days of school, I asked my mom for a necklace; she eventually figured out I was looking for a rosary. We would pray the rosary together on Fridays in second grade, or as a whole school, such as when 9/11 happened. We headed our papers with the letters "J.M.J.L.A." for Jesus, Mary, Joseph, St. Lucy, and St. Anthony. We learned the stories of Jesus.

We went to Masson the first Friday of the month, with a group of us acting as altar servers, lectors, and cantors. I was one of my principal's go-to's as a lector to read a selection from the Bible or special intentions for the congregation to pray for. During Lent, the season of preparation for Easter, we would skip recess to go to Mass and participate in the Stations of the Cross, which chronicle Jesus' passion, crucifixion, and death.

My grade school was referred to as being "in the basement of a church" since it was built a floor below the church. This worked because classroom sizes in Catholic schools tend to be smaller than those in public schools and with fewer classes per grade. I had 16 students on average in my class in grade school. A smaller school meant that the older students had more opportunities to help younger students as mentors and helpers. However, smaller classrooms, while beneficial for tight-knit learning experiences, do not bode well when the teacher is harsh or you don't happen to fit in with your classmates.

Bullying

My first experience of bullying happened in second grade, when I admitted to some classmates that I still liked *Sesame Street,* and they laughed at me. Most of the bullying, which predominantly happened from second grade to early high school, was emotional. It entailed comments about what I wore, what I brought to lunch, and how I went about my life. When I had roommates who teased and questioned me in my early adulthood, it felt similar, despite the jabs coming from very different places.

There were rarely issues in the bathroom, although I can recall two bullying incidents originating there. In third grade, my peers looked at the stall I was in to find that I had accidentally peed on the toilet seat, having been too lazy to raise it up. They proceeded to make fun of me to the point that I was left crying in the back of my class. The teacher noticed and had them apologize to me for the incident, although I felt most of their apologies to be disingenuous. By age 8, I had already grown distrustful of my peers.

In third or fourth grade when my class had a pizza party, the boys went to the bathroom. As we left, my peers slammed the door shut on me. While it was a little cruel and annoying, I figured that once they let go of the door, I could leave. The school had recently repainted the bathroom door, though, and upon it being shut with force, it became stuck.

Unable to push it open, I screamed for help, my voice echoing off the tiled lavatory walls that looked like they belonged more in an asylum than a grade school bathroom. A teacher heard me through a window outside where the older kids were having recess.

"Stop yelling!" she said back to me, ignoring my pleas for help.

I teared up alone in my despair and proceeded to yell again.

"Help!"

"What!?" the teacher annoyingly replied.

"I'm stuck," I mustered through tears.

This time the teacher sent an older student who opened the door with ease. I was free. I made the walk of shame back to the pizza party.

Significant, specific incidents of bullying besides these elude me. Take the analogy of a football player who has a concussion versus a player who doesn't, but who experiences many bumps and hits over time. While both players had head trauma, one experienced it in one shot while the other's occurred over time. Getting frequent bumps to the head, day after day, is what my bullying experience felt like.

Bullying was the moments of being told to shut up when I would attempt to tell a joke, or when someone threw a quarter into my thermos and then made fun of me for still eating the soup in it. It was getting called out for a new accessory my mom sent me to school with, like a pocket protector or a book strap to hold my books together while we stood outside a classroom. It was someone taking my seat at the lunch table or ridiculing me when I attempted to stand up for myself despite being outnumbered.

I felt left out of plans to ride bikes or play football in the neighborhood. I felt rejected for not getting passed the ball or getting to throw it during sports.

Sometimes, I would spend the whole recess or gym class waiting to get the ball just once, only for a stronger kid to rip it out of my hands when I finally got it.

The Teachers

Meanwhile, some of my grade school teachers were among the angriest, most controlling individuals I ever met. I'm surprised they were not reported for their frequent emotional abuse toward students. They would reprimand us for even the most minor infraction, such as talking in class or speaking out of line.

Worse, they actively shamed every student. A low grade on a test would be announced aloud, sometimes with the disapproving feedback of the teacher. Difficulty with a math problem or failure to complete homework was ridiculed, oftentimes with the student having to stand at the board helplessly as the rest of the class watched. Any creative thought outside the parameters of what the teachers said was considered blasphemy.

I felt bullied by the teachers as much as the students. The seventh- and eighth-grade classes were typically combined because of the school's size constraints and the fact that most of the content overlapped.

At one point, a school newspaper was developed, the same newspaper that was debunked by a family friend years prior (the same friend whose book inspired the structure of this one). I was proud of my contributions and excited to see my work in the finished product. Much to my disappointment, my last name was misspelled.

Throughout my life, I've become used to my name being mispronounced and misspelled. Capoccia, an Italian name meaning "head of a peasant family," according to Cambridge dictionary, is pronounced *Cah-poe-chee*. I became frustrated and eventually apathetic to the increasingly creative mispronunciations. My last name holds importance to me, and in a way, it validates my subtle sense of leadership. I was annoyed.

I took it upon myself to speak my mind. I assertively asked to speak privately with my teacher and the two editors of the school paper, pretty yet intimidating eighth-grade girls.

"My name was misspelled in the paper, which hurt me, and I would like a new version printed with my last name corrected," I said.

With pushback, the teacher rebutted, "These girls have worked so hard on this paper, and this is how you thank them? I don't think this is appropriate behavior, Mr. Capoccia."

Her defensiveness and the use of my last name caught me off guard. I had already used every bit of courage I had to initiate this conversation, and I had none left to finish it. I ended up crying and instead, apologized to them.

Ultimately, one of the girls made it a point to find out how to properly spell my name, sharing the helpful tip to double the "c," not the "p." Dissimilarly, conversations with the other girl felt condescending thereafter, and I loathed when she would confront me.

However, the damage from this moment was done. I believe a wound was formed that day, accompanied by a vow that I would never assert myself for how I felt. I doubted people would listen and felt instead that they would use my feelings against me. My people-pleasing tendencies were fueled by my fear of the guilt and shame I felt that day.

I've long held resentment toward these teachers as deeply, if not more deeply, than the peers who bullied me. I wouldn't expect a bunch of my childhood bullies, with their own upbringings and childhood issues, to have acted differently. But the teachers were adults — they don't get a pass.

Many of my peers may have had learning disabilities, ADHD, or autism. We had outsiders who observed and heard of the teachers' behaviors, including a speech pathologist, special education staff, office staff, priests, nuns, and our own parents. During the 1990s and early 2000s, this sort of teaching practice was still deemed normal. Both my parents encouraged me to stand up for myself, which did not have the desired outcome. They stood up to these teachers on occasion, but this didn't stop the problems. I feared the teachers and the backlash.

Making Sense of Childhood

Much of my childhood felt like a battleground — me against the boys in my class, my classmates and me against the teachers, my mother against the school. I wasn't like my peers. I had difficulty connecting with the boys and girls in my class, feeling on the outskirts of both groups. I wondered why that was. From a young age, I knew what activities were important to me, and they rarely involved my classmates, like bowling, piano, and video games.

I wondered if I was too sensitive growing up, that the boys teased me as initiation into their friend group. Or did I truly not fit in, with my defensiveness leading to more mockery? I still can't tell if I was developmentally more mature or less mature than my classmates. My mom told me that at parties with family friends, I'd hold intelligent conversations with the adults. Meanwhile, I couldn't seem to grasp how to interact with the kids. I was socialized to be more independent, but part of me simply wanted to fit in. I truly wanted to belong.

Another difference between me and my classmates, which I realized later in life, was socioeconomic status. I grew up as a lower-middle class kid at a Catholic school where many of the other students' families had money and houses that were much larger than mine. My classmates had their own bedrooms, while I shared one with my brother. And while their families often had two floors of living space, mine had just the second floor of our home while my grandparents lived on the first. I didn't wear name-brand clothes, and I wasn't taught to brag. My parents gave me everything I needed and most of what I wanted.

From home, my mom would discourage me from joining sports because of a heart condition I had from a young age and from joining school events if she didn't feel it necessary for us to go. Often, these would be attending a Mass or participating in a silly performance. I don't know if I cared to do those things either, but I wanted to belong. And in a school where teachers openly shamed any form of defecting, I would be heavily questioned for not attending.

What's Mental Health?

My first experience with what I believe was depression came at age 13, likely the result of a combination of hormones, a sinus infection, and seasonal depression. I had another sinus infection not long after this, which affected my eating to the point that twice in a short period of time, I got sick at restaurants, one of which was a pizza place. I developed a fear of going to restaurants and avoided certain foods such as pizza and sandwiches. I worried frequently about eating in general. What ensued was years of anxiety that I realize now stemmed from obsessions — fixations on particular thoughts, a key component of obsessive compulsive disorder (OCD).

Throughout my preteen and early teen years, I would obsess frequently about what I was going to eat that day, whether it was what my mom packed in my lunch or what was for dinner. Lunchtime was the worst part of my day — the time when I was forced to interact with my classmates who would inevitably make fun of me. Multiple times during eighth grade, I got sick at lunch or left early to go home to eat lunch there and watch the NFL Network. I felt comforted watching Rich Eisen and my childhood hero, Terrell Davis.

Growing up in the '90s and early 2000s, I didn't know what mental health was. While these worries I experienced became a nightmare, they were an ordinary part of my life. I don't think I realized my mind wasn't meant to work this way, and it wasn't something I discussed with my family or friends, let alone a trained professional.

I disliked dealing with many of my classmates. I should have told my mom I hated the school and demanded to be homeschool, sent to the other Catholic school down the street, or transferred to a public school. Any of those options couldn't have been worse than where I was.

A need for validation, feeling defensive about others making fun of me, and believing that I was not enough and didn't belong have followed me from this six-year period. They've unknowingly influenced many aspects of my life. It's hard to shake the damage that happened during this critical time.

I can assure you that I've healed from and processed many of these experiences. The feeling of not belonging has actually allowed me to find one of my greatest spiritual gifts — showing mercy. I am a fairly nonjudgmental person and am competent in socializing with people from various backgrounds and belief systems. I learned my inherent value as a child of God.

Not fitting in helped me gain an adaptable ability to adjust to the people and environments I encountered. I didn't get stuck in a group or clique, so I became a chameleon. The drawback of being a chameleon, though, is not knowing what color you actually are.

The unfortunate part of my grade school experience was that I carried much of this alone. I did not attend counseling, let alone knew anyone who did. I certainly needed it for anxiety and OCD. My parents knew about the bullying, worries about eating, and overall feeling of not belonging. They would offer advice or encouragement and loved me greatly, but they were too close to the situation. I was thankful for the friends I had outside of school so I could get away from that environment, but we did not talk about school or my mental health. I lacked emotional awareness, therapeutic or peer support, and the ability/environment to communicate. It's by the grace of God I was given the opportunities to learn enough about myself to help others.

I held far more anger than anyone knew, including me. Denial became a best friend. It might surprise people to learn about the deep resentments this quiet, kind-hearted nerd held. That anger comes back sometimes, but now I know how to wield or defuse it.

Insight: "Audience at a Concert"

One of my favorite analogies to describe mindfulness is that of a rock concert. Let's say you're playing in a band as a concert is ending. Some fans are cheering, others are booing; some are yelling for an encore, and one drunk guy in the back is yelling for "Free Bird." A mixed crowd. Similarly, our thoughts can rush with approval, disapproval, suggestions, and nonsense. Regardless of what the band hears, they can choose to play another song, walk off the stage, or contest the booing. They could entertain the "Free Bird" guy or ignore him and half the crowd.

I wish I had known of this analogy in light of the peer bullying and the mental/emotional abuse from my teachers. The band doesn't have to take ownership of what happens at the concert. It doesn't have to internalize it as a reflection of its performance or identity. A famous one-liner describes this well: "A thought is just a thought."

It can be difficult at first to wrap your mind around the fact that your thoughts aren't necessarily yours and that they aren't necessarily true. Random thoughts run through our minds daily. Some are helpful, well-timed, and insightful. Others are intrusive, obsessive, or even disturbing. We get to choose which we engage with and use to our benefit and which we may fight, reframe, or ignore.

Take the thought, "I have a million dollars." This thought doesn't mean you now have a million dollars, and the thought alone doesn't make it happen. If you desire to make this thought a reality, you may have to set goals or change priorities. Or if you're so fortunate, you may already have a million dollars, but the thought didn't make it so.

Fears and intrusive thoughts may be experienced, but the thoughts don't make the words a reality. We can believe thoughts that we are unworthy or unloveable, but even as strongly as we may believe them, which could lead to a number of negative outcomes, they are not true. For some, fighting these thoughts with real-world evidence can be helpful. For others, allowing the thoughts to move along and manage the distress associated with them instead may be more effective.

Who Is God?

I learned the basics about God in my childhood — that He loved me, and through my relationship with Him, I was to love others. On Saturday evenings or Sunday mornings, my family went to Mass together. God was a part of my life through school, my family, and Scouts. When I knelt down in church at my first Communion, I thanked God for so long that a classmate alerted me to sit back down for the closing prayer. There was a fervor in this experience I can't explain for my age.

My next-door neighbor, Robert, had muscular dystrophy. I visited him from time to time, as he was bedridden or in a wheelchair. He loved pigs and had a huge collection of pig-related items throughout his home. He also collected stickers from his doctor's appointments that nearly filled the family fridge. Despite his situation, he was always smiling. He passed away as a preteen, far too young. From a young age, I understood him to be my guardian angel, that he was looking over me. I didn't feel sad when he passed but rather saw him journeying with me differently.

Finding Friends

Good friends kept me afloat as I entered my preteen years. Academically, I ranked fourth in my class of 16 students, and at sports, I typically was picked last or second-to-last. But bowling was where I was accepted and belonged. People my age talked with me like I was a "normal" kid, wanted me on their teams, and applauded my talent. I was one of the best in the leagues for most of my childhood, which was validating. I was treated with kindness, respect, and even admiration.

The internet, meanwhile, led to an important friendship. It was the early days of the web when dial-up internet meant slow refresh speeds, limited time online, and clogging up the phone lines. My brother and I became fans of the *Animal Crossing* series following a hangout with my godfather's son, who was an older brother-type figure growing up. Games he recommended often became favorites in my household, and later in life, books he authored became some of my favorites, too. The structure of this book was inspired by one of his, *Mega Man 3*. From my love for *Animal Crossing*, I became involved with a website called Animal Crossing Community (ACC).

Through the site, I began building online friendships, including one which led to a year-and-a-half-long relationship that went into high school. Like me, she enjoyed video games, football, and psychology. We talked about our days, and I looked forward to messaging on AOL Instant Messenger (AIM) and replying to paragraphs of emails. On occasion, we talked on the phone. Hearing her voice — someone my age telling me how much she cared for me — was what I needed at a time when I felt undervalued by my peers.

She lived in South Carolina, and we never met in person. Both our parents had frequent worries about the other, and rightly so. We were preteens talking over the internet in an age when it was fairly easy to remain anonymous. Either of us could have been predators. My parents often argued with me about this relationship and my online time, with my mom going so far as to deny that it was a relationship. To me, though, it was. It was the strongest relationship or friendship I had as a child or pre-teen. I'm thankful I had her.

Chapter Three
High School

A Fresh Start

I began to find myself in high school. I wanted to start fresh and knew I had something to prove. And so when situations arose that mirrored those from grade school, I chose to take a different direction.

Initially, I sat at a lunch table with some of my old classmates from grade school. When I would leave my lunchbag to run to the bathroom, one student would steal my Reese's pieces. I considered various pranks to stop him, including coating the bag in Sharpie marker, but instead wrote the commandment, "Thou shalt not steal" on a sticky note. Laughter erupted as I went to the bathroom, but it didn't make me feel ashamed like it would have a year prior. Instead, I felt convicted that I no longer had to deal with such treatment. I moved tables shortly after and joined a new group of friends.

One student who bullied me throughout grade school, seemingly making my experience miserable single-handedly, said mean or disturbing things to me even in high school. His attempts to rattle me weren't so rattling, though, and years later, we ended up at the same college, where I offered him help. Instead of judgment, I chose kindness, which I'm far more proud of.

Team B

Throughout high school, I used bowling primarily to remake myself. My goal was to have bowling recognized not as a club but as a sport. One of the nuns at the school, the late Sister Amy, was our moderator and coach for my freshman season, and she had a similar goal to me. Bowling worked differently than the other high school sports since we had multiple teams, one for every four or five bowlers who signed up. Sometimes bowlers were grouped by who was friends with whom, as bowling was designated more for fun than competition.

Sister Amy took our highest-average bowlers and created the "B" team. By the spring season, we had won our first championship. A senior, Chris, who was like a mentor to me and has since passed, picked me up and spun me around following our victory, to which Sister Amy emphatically shouted, "Chris, put Ross down!" My best friend's father was one of the founding members of the league we bowled in, and he was quite proud of our championship win.

In my junior year, during which my high school merged with another and changed its name, we won another championship. This was, to my knowledge, the first sports championship in the newly merged high school's history. While we experienced championship losses, too, the wins made the defeats unimportant.

Bowling offered me the sense of belonging and community I struggled to find in the classroom. I formed some of my closest high school friendships through bowling. My friends accepted me for who I was, even when I was difficult to handle. I was a tryhard, to say the least, pushing my teammates even when they did not need a nudge. I admittedly took some of the joy and excitement away from these experiences that now I wish I appreciated more. There are few seasons in my life when I have laughed as much as I did with those teams, or felt that I belonged to something greater the way I did with them.

I received a "most valuable player" award for bowling in each of my four years of high school, and in some small way, I contributed to my ultimate goal of bowling being recognized as a sport. Awareness began in small ways, such as through announcements of our victories being read over the intercom. Students and teachers began to care about when we won and even visited the lanes to see what the hype was about. The school paid for uniforms and later offered transportation to matches, even paying some of the funds for the students to bowl. These amenities often are taken for granted in other sports, but for us, we had to work for them.

My brother became the best bowler the school ever had. My mother was influential as a coach in forming a strong coaching staff, advocating for her bowlers, and building relationships with the administration and league. I joined them as a coach for a season early in college, and some of my bowlers qualified for a statewide tournament. The tradition of the "B" team continued into my brother's high school years, with the school taking multiple bowling championships.

Friends and, I Guess, School

Academics came easily to me. I ensured I had free blocks for study hall rather than taking Latin class my junior and senior years to make school work even easier. The less homework at home, the better. My academic goal was to score high enough grades to not take the final exams. I did minimal work, and few classes challenged me enough to study, which proved concerning when I started college.

High school was primarily a time when I learned how to make friends. My best friend for much of high school was kind-hearted and funny. He was bigger and taller than me, which made for an odd-couple dynamic. We bowled together, and he treated me as an equal. His love for REO Speedwagon became contagious as we'd jam out on car rides, and he was passionate about his mother's Camaro that he worked on himself. While we argued at times over girls or bowling, we spent a good amount of time in high school attached at the hip. We called each other frequently and spent our summers together, getting to know each other's families in the process. He taught me that I was likable and worth having around as a friend, even when I was difficult or a perfectionist.

In high school, the smarter kids tend to get accolades, the troublemakers get punished, and the rest — the average students, the smart kids who let their grades fall out of boredom, the students who struggle with math and English but could paint a mural or fix your car — fall through the cracks. I saw this in my own friends: one who was caring but struggled to keep up academically, and another who was a genius but fell into drugs, boredom, and apathy. Neither seemed to draw the school's concern. This bothered me to the point that I set a goal of becoming a school psychologist with the intention of helping high school teens like my friends who fell through the cracks.

My online relationship continued into high school. Others caught on, noticing my AIM profile with a heart next to her name or hearing about my relationship through close friends. I felt ostracized for this, and rightly so. It was a strange time to have an online girlfriend. I started developing romantic interests at school, even flirting with a crush. I should have realized dating a girl I never met from a state I'd never been to wouldn't work.

She distanced herself from me for a week and then email me about us breaking up. This devastated me. From reviewing my old journals, my love and grief surrounding her were strong. There felt like a lack of closure, especially since we had never met — as though we truly did not receive the chance to explore a love and life together thanks to our ages and the distance separating us. As an adult, I understand this complexity in dating, but teenage me certainly did not.

Am I Going Crazy?

Some of the building blocks of OCD seemed to take shape in me as a teenager. For example, I was obsessed with bowling to the extent that I thought about our matches every week and looked for opportunities to promote the sport in the school even when it wasn't warranted. I frequently pushed my bowling teams to win, even when they tried their best or emphasized to me that winning wasn't the most important thing to them. I was hyperfixated on the sport.

Meanwhile, my school environment was rigid, from the Catholic school uniforms to the morality we learned to the way discipline was instilled. Religion and theology classes unfortunately focused less on our relationships with God and more on the guidelines and rules of the Catholic Church without the proper connection back to a personal journey with God. I believe this to be one of the greatest failings of a Catholic education. Rules and explanations on how to follow teachings of a religion are indeed valuable, although this must not be at the expense of a relationship with God. It should be a way to form and build a relationship. I adopted this scrupulosity and communicated that in conversations with friends.

Additionally, I formed certain personality traits and behaviors. I was very organized, which proved to be helpful with my planner at school or in my work organizing books at a local library. I used spreadsheets frequently to label the video games my brother and I owned, or to make other arbitrary lists. I ruminated often about crushes and opportunities for talking to girls I liked. While none of these by themselves substantiated an OCD diagnosis, they certainly became maladaptive when done too much or in the wrong situations.

Building Blocks of Faith

My faith in high school seemed small. I wanted to be a good person, and I went to Mass on weekends and at school. I sang in my church's choir for a time until I overheard some girls joking about singing in a deeper voice. Considering I was the only guy in the choir, I figured they were making fun of me and stopped attending. They might not have been talking about me or making fun of me at all, but my defenses were up, and I opted to avoid the situation.

I believed in God and enjoyed having conversations with close friends about God's existence. However, I didn't have a personal relationship with God. God felt "out there" versus "right here." Theology and morality were at the center of my Christian conversations, rather than how to become closer to God or how to read His Word in the Bible. I could not say I knew His promises or had built a trust in Him thanks to that significant shortcoming in Catholic education — the overemphasis on theology and morality to the detriment of learning the basic Christian tenets of building a loving, faith-filled relationship with God, others, and ourselves.

I came across this quote from a story I had begun writing when I was 16, which leads me to believe that faith held importance even then: "The whole scheme of things resembled dark, malevolent upbringings and cross-bearing undertakings, but faith helped us through the day."

Insight: Counseling & Faith

I've found that religion and spirituality can be the best healing for mental health. My own faith experiences have brought the most healing to my mental health issues. Likewise, I've seen among my clients that those who are more religious or spiritual tend to have more hope and heal faster. This does not seem to be a coincidence. If we frame life in terms of our relationship with God, it's no wonder so many wander and suffer.

But there is a reason for receiving mental health treatment even when religion and spirituality are available to us. We are stewards of our minds, as we are stewards of the bodies and souls we were given. Understanding and identifying our tendencies — their positive and shadow sides — allows us to be better for God, others, and ourselves. Healing from past hurts allows us to let love back in as "God is love" (1 John 4:8). Our perspectives sometimes need to be widened, our expectations and assumptions challenged, our narratives reframed, our vices held in check, and our hearts healed. This is where therapy assists a disciple to live out their faith.

Counseling also can offer the groundedness we need to pursue our faith. There can be times when we pursue purpose so wholeheartedly that we lose track of what's in front of us or "the next best thing," as my former spiritual director would say. For people like me whose mental rulebooks are a little too strict, a therapist who is spiritually aware can help loosen the binds we put on ourselves. These often are arbitrary rules that God didn't put on us.

My guidance for faith-based therapists is to watch when clients may be lost in their faith rather than free in it. And for those therapists who are not attached to a religion or spirituality, be careful not to drag people away from faith as you address their mental health issues. The goal is to help clients deal with their mental health within the context of their faith or spirituality.

For example, I had to learn the skill of separating what my OCD thought was important, what I think is important, and what God thinks is important. This process of identifying these individually is discernment. I had to reflect and confront some of my Catholic guilt. This allowed for a more forgiving way to see my relationship with God, rather than a harsh way that traced my issues to my childhood Catholic education. Reintroducing previous faith-based rituals, such as the rosary and attending Mass, came later, as they required me to reflect and work on some resentment in order to move forward.

Recognizing God's healing of wounds became critical for my spiritual and mental health journeys.

Play Me the Blues: First Rejection

I didn't realize the wounds I suffered in high school until later. One painful instance that stands out happened at a talent show during my junior year. Having signed up to play a song on the piano in front of the school, I told my crush about my upcoming performance. She excitedly told me she wanted a song dedicated to her. Me being a hopeless romantic, I signed up to do a second song.

Upon entering the stage, I announced over the microphone to the whole school who the song was for. The performance was incredible, as the student body sang along while I played. However, when I went to leave school that day, there was no sign of my crush, no one waiting for me with open arms and heart afire. Instead, I heard through a friend of a friend that she was "mortified." We never talked about it. This was my first experience of rejection.

I asked her out, the first time I asked anyone on a date, a couple months later. We made loose plans that Saturday morning, but I didn't hear from her for the rest of the weekend. Another rejection.

One day in Latin class, a short girl with jet-black hair arrived. Her shoes and purse suggested she was into punk or Goth. I couldn't tell. It didn't matter to me. I fell for her instantly. We had a mutual friend, and I got her AIM screen name. We messaged each other frequently and sometimes met before homeroom to walk the school. However, she wanted a guy who played the guitar, and I was a nerd who played the piano.

I later found myself pursuing a cheerleader. She sat behind me in chemistry class. Her eyes had the most beautiful irises I had ever seen. Her freckles highlighted her face. I got the courage to turn around to talk to her and even began tutoring her to have an excuse to chat. Once, she even came over to my house to study for a chemistry final. We ended up sitting on my bedroom floor, playing *Nintendogs*, our faces cheek to cheek smiling at the virtual puppies, before she had to leave. She showed interest from time to time, but whenever we got more serious, she backed away.

My senior year, I met a sweet brunette girl who loved to read. We quickly became close, and I made my first big move since the talent show, kissing her on the cheek. She acted aloof toward me, though, and when I questioned her, I learned she did not want a serious relationship until college. A few months later, she had found her person, and they were a couple I couldn't deny was a match.

Years later, I realized I carried these wounds of rejection. I feared being direct with women when I was interested, unknowingly making a vow not to put myself in the position of potentially being hurt by a girl without knowing her intentions. I wanted more certainty in dating and romance than a person needed, which had its own drawbacks.

Senior Year: A Strange Start to a Chapter's End

Senior year can be stressful to begin with — being the oldest students at the school, attending major events like award ceremonies and prom, taking the SATs, applying for college, and saying goodbye to a chapter of life. It is a time marked by profound change, with the big fish in a small pond getting cast out into a world where high school achievements become fairly meaningless.

Meanwhile, I continued dealing with my aforementioned worries about eating, working at the local library, and preparing for a college course I ultimately dropped because of my mental health.

My senior year in particular was unique. Thanks to the school merger, my class was to be the new school's first graduates. I wasn't looking forward to starting the school year, as I wouldn't know over half of the students, and my OCD became more pronounced that summer before school started.

I feared an obsessive, intrusive thought that if I scored points on a quiz or test, I wouldn't be able to eat. I don't quite understand how this made sense in my mind. Ultimately, I wasn't scared of grades but rather the uncertainty — so much uncertainty — but my OCD brain couldn't process that. I knew I had to succeed in high school.

One incident challenged this obsession in a strange way. A classmate from the other high school from the merger who sat behind me in physics class purposely filled out a quiz with all the wrong answers. At the top of the quiz, he wrote my name in terrible handwriting. I was perturbed, as was my physics teacher, but I eventually found the humor and cleverness in it. This bizarre incident calmed me down. The initial anger I felt expressed to me how much I truly did care about good grades. I gained the opportunity to see first-hand what it would have been like if I complied with my intrusive thoughts and sabotaged my academics. Humor helped against my OCD.

However, my OCD didn't stop there. Throughout the year, I caught myself reading sentences over and over. I started thinking the same thoughts repetitively to get them "right," even to the point of making myself sick with anxiety. At night when I'd go to sleep in a bunk bed I shared with my brother, I repetitively stepped on and off the bottom step of the ladder in the dark, hoping not to wake him.

The worst of these symptoms subsided as I adjusted to my new high school, yet my overall mental health gradually grew more concerning in the background. Despite the status of my underlying OCD, I had a positive senior year. I made many new friends, with my friend group mostly consisting of guys from my original high school and girls from the other one. A core of this group became some of my closest friends a few years into our undergraduate studies.

They didn't know what I was going through, nor did it occur to me that I could reveal my fears to them.

Events overall went well for me that year as I won my fourth "most valuable player" award for bowling, was voted one of the best singers at Class Day, and finished with the eighth-highest GPA in my combined class (sixth among those from my original high school).

Graduation took place at the gym of my future college, Marywood University. Exiting the front doors of the commencement venue, I was at my college campus, what would become my second home for the next seven and a half years.

Chapter Four
Home Away From Home
Undergrad

"I'm Sorry, I'm a Freshman. I Didn't Know."

This was the phrase a speaker at orientation humorously taught the hundreds of us new to the college experience as our free pass to get out of the problems he anticipated we would have. As a commuter, I'd go to class then leave for work or go straight home. I didn't feel I had much independence or choice. My nose was to the proverbial grindstone, taking my academics seriously. I'd spend morning breaks in my college's rotunda doing homework and unintentional people watching, looking up from *The Iliad* and my notepad of annotations to notice a passerby.

Occasionally, I met with some students from my major and attended events on-campus, such as live music or comedy shows. Meanwhile, I bowled in a youth league with my brother on Saturday mornings. However, I rarely saw my high school friends, who were scattered at various colleges, some local, some farther away.

Admittedly, I was unprepared for college. I had skated through K-12 with little struggle, but I came into college with little reading, studying, or organizational skills. I didn't know how to balance the workload I had, ask for help, or properly prepare for an exam. What I lacked academically, accompanied by an ego built from years of easy classes, set the stage for my biggest breakdown.

What I learned quickly about the simple mantra communicated at freshmen orientation was that I was indeed a freshman, and I didn't know.

Winter Break Meltdown

I initially earned good grades my first semester, but my OCD was becoming debilitating. When I read for classes, I had trouble getting past even a few sentences of material without using compulsions. Reading sentences over and over until I said them "right" in my mind became commonplace. I wasn't comprehending the content or reading fast enough to keep up with the pace of college, so I gave up on reading. I found acceptable ways to skim over material. It didn't prove effective.

My first finals week was a disaster. I failed my statistics final. I spent most of that final erasing, rewriting, and erasing answers again, knowing full well that I didn't know how to solve the problems. I felt ashamed and defeated, emotions I hadn't experienced in academics, having previously excelled with little to no effort. Additionally, I had bonded with the professor and truly believed I had let him down. I had carried an A into the final before receiving a 44 on the exam, which accounted for forty percent of my overall grade. I was convinced this exam would cause me to lose my scholarship. Instead, I finished the class with a generous B-.

My other finals went poorly as well, including a Spanish one I understood very little of and a general psych final in which I missed an entire page of questions and got an A-, a tie for my lowest psychology grade.

I obsessed about how I let down my statistics professor. While a 3.3 GPA to start college would be quite acceptable for most people, I was devastated. I spent the winter break of 2009 at rock bottom. I'd wake up in the morning dreading the day, knowing how awful it would be to have to do the same compulsive rituals over and over.

Showering at night took me almost an hour, as I had to follow the arbitrary rules involved for undressing, entering the shower, showering, dressing, and throwing away the cotton swabs I used. Throwing out something was next to impossible without me having to pick it up and drop it back in the trash can, sometimes trying to say a certain word in my mind when I discarded the item or thinking of a particular friend.

My parents gave me pep talks, and my mom was convinced that using a timer helped me. It did give me some incentive to move faster, but I was so trapped in the obsessions that ultimately it didn't matter. I watched *Rocky* movies, my only source of motivation besides my parents that gave me hope. The world had certainly knocked me down.

I felt scared that I wouldn't get through the next semester and would stay this way. I didn't want to think about where I would end up in this condition. My parents even worried about letting me drive for fear that I would let my obsessions and compulsions take over.

I distinctly remember spending way too much time creating a Christmas card on the computer, making sure every word was typed a certain way and the graphics were perfectly aligned. I hit the print button and proceeded to fold the card over and over, the creases becoming wider and deeper until my brother yelled at me as he noticed what was happening. That's where the most shame comes from — not only letting myself down every time I gave into my inner fears and worries, but also when someone I loved saw me in this state. I knew it scared and hurt them, too.

Family Guilt

If I have any regret about my OCD, it is that my family, and my brother specifically, had to endure it. I felt ashamed when he would notice my compulsions. This occurred during a bizarre bedtime ritual to check for scorpions and spiders. I got stuck in a loop. I shined my flashlight back and forth, on the sides of my bed, under the covers, over and over for what felt like minutes. He screamed at me to stop, and it jolted me into doing so.

I never talked to him about this moment, or about the Christmas card folding, or about how he had to vicariously take on my many mental health issues. These included the times I wouldn't go to a party because of worries about eating or the compulsions he saw me experience.

Sometimes I feel guilty he had to deal with my mental health issues. I also know that these issues weren't my fault and that, as a teenager, I barely knew how to deal with them myself. If he reads my book, it may be the first time he finds out what I was going through or how I felt. My parents taught me from a young age to protect my younger brother, but my OCD couldn't care less about this responsibility.

Intro to Counseling 101

My mom called my college's counseling center over the Christmas break, and the director, Dr. Robert Shaw, said he would see me. He was a larger man with the stature of a bear and a slight smile that seemed imprinted on his face below an impressive mustache. He served as a psychologist, and I came to learn that he was also a reverend.

Dr. Shaw's words were intentional and thoughtful, his cadence slow. I shared from time to time but mostly found myself listening intently to what he had to say. Perhaps it was his speech that offered me a moment of calm, a voice that could serenade a baby to sleep.

I was ashamed to be there, though. "I'm a psychology major! I'm the one who's supposed to be helping others. I'm not supposed to be the one who needs help!" I ignorantly thought to myself. I was a proud, cocky eighteen-year-old, misguided to believe life was full of easily attainable achievements and trophies, and that one misstep would shake the world.

"You can't sit in *this* chair until you've sat in *that* chair," Dr. Shaw pointed out to me, signaling from his seat to mine.

This meant I needed to go through my own suffering to help others.

Insight: "You Can't Sit in *This* Chair Until You've Sat in *That* Chair"

Therapy is healing for both the traveler and the guide. Counseling can be compared to a seedling that represents larger roots, a lifestyle of health, growth, and being. Your participation in counseling as a person who values self care, whether as a therapist or someone else, is much like the participation of a yoga instructor who exercises, a financial advisor who invests, or a nutritionist who eats healthily. Personal counseling gives us an hour to put the spotlight on our individual journeys.

There is no shame in going to therapy. Many people may see therapy as a personal failing or a last resort. While it is a vulnerable choice to attend, it is not a weak one. Participating in therapy shows a sense of humility, wisdom, and acceptance that one cannot solve one's own problems. Admittedly, therapy is difficult, but going without it when it is needed is far tougher.

We are relational creatures, born into this world highly dependent upon others. Compare humans to other animals, and you'll see how dependent we truly are. We need God, significant others, family, friends, and community, especially during a time when our world appears to be more fragmented and disconnected. Counseling is signing up to have the opportunity for this bond with a trained professional who may act as a bridge in connecting you more deeply with others.

Meanwhile, clients can take solace knowing that therapists have their own stories. Whether you realize it or not, many therapists do the work of therapy because it is part of the fabric of their own stories, that they may have suffered from (or still deal with) mental health issues and life struggles. Furthermore, the healing power of therapy may have significantly impacted therapists' own lives, which led them to pursue work in the field and share their knowledge with others. This great desire to help others may have come from a broken place, meaning that the therapist you see likely understands more than techniques and diagnoses — they understand brokenness and hope. Taking responsibility for their own problems and being aware of their own light and darkness is a gift therapists can pass onto others.

Therapy is not a field people join for surface-level reasons, such as to gain great status or wealth, or because it was the only job available. Our field is different from many others in this respect. To understand their jobs, the surgeon doesn't need to be operated on, the police officer doesn't have to get arrested, and the wedding planner doesn't have to be married. But consider the empathy and understanding professionals in other fields might add to their work if they've received what they've offered.

It's crucial to remember that, at its core, stripped of the structure, status, and boundaries, counseling can be boiled down to a conversation. Talk. Observe. Experience. Connect. This is where you can be cognizant of your interventions and ethics, of course, but remain grounded in your own, genuine self and the relationship between therapist and client.

As a client, I've wondered about my therapists' personal lives, texted them at inappropriate hours, sent gratitude letters when I was no longer their client, dropped "bombs" at the end of a session, asked for their opinions, and wanted their approval deeply. As much as I love God, my family, and my friends, I needed my therapists. My experience as a client helps me better understand my own.

Freedom From the Cage

Just as valuable, Dr. Shaw instructed me that, "You have to put the saddle on the horse." This speaks to managing qualities within oneself. Analogously, before a wild horse is broken and gets its saddle, it runs with no restraint in whatever direction it pleases. Meanwhile, a horse with a saddle that has undergone training and built trust can serve as an excellent transporter and a happy companion. Likewise, qualities within ourselves can run amok or benefit us greatly. In terms of OCD, I can present as obsessive, controlling, overthinking, and hypervigilant. However, those same qualities can help me be meticulous, conscientious, careful, detail-oriented, and thoughtful. It took years for me to realize that OCD wasn't simply a disorder but a reflection of how my mind worked.

During one emotional session, Dr. Shaw played "Amazing Grace" and leaned over to me as I cried to acknowledge that he "rattled my cage." He certainly had — I was understood. I rarely told him what the actual problems were in my mind. Perhaps I feared judgment, maybe I thought I was crazy, but most of all, I feared the OCD itself. I thought if I revealed the mechanics of its devilish tasks, I would serve the repercussions. This too was an obsession, and it kept me from connecting with one of the greatest therapists I've ever sat across from. Despite my dodging and vague statements, he knew what to say and the path I needed to be on.

Dr. Shaw once cleverly pivoted our conversation to God and how He could help me. I believed in God most of my life and went to Catholic school, and instilling fear of going to hell for sin was a tactic with which I was well familiar. But the idea that I could have a personal relationship with God was new and different. "Trust in God" was the mantra my therapist coined for me. It was clear Dr. Shaw was tactful in his approach, and he found the right moment. God was there the whole time in plain sight.

Winter Blues Bring Spring Refuge

When I felt the urge to engage in a compulsion, I instead thought of the mantra Dr. Shaw developed, and it helped. I spent one semester working with him, and I felt "cured." More importantly, though, I saw how God could change my life.

The spring semester of college was a breath of fresh air compared to the doom of the first one. I spent time preparing for class and learned the necessary skills to succeed in college. I actually enjoyed it — the structure, the learning, the social interaction. I slowly began to make friends but still spent more time at home than on campus.

I completed counseling the spring of my freshmen year. I was so eager to be finished, I wasn't aware of my discharge appointment. A week following my missed session, Dr. Shaw explained to both my parents and me that based on the psychological testing he had done when I first arrived, that I had lost the "fight" in me. However, on another graph, he showed how I had regained it. He referred to my symptoms as an "OCD track," the first time my symptoms were clinically recognized as being tied to OCD. Using the phrase "OCD track," however, gave me the impression I did not actually have OCD itself. My issues were temporary and, at that point, gone.

Looking back, I realize that therapy shouldn't have stopped there. I got to the point I refer to as "the hump," the place where the client is no longer stuck in the worst of their problems. However, there are still issues to tackle, insight to gain, and growth to experience. Sometimes people don't want more from treatment, and that has to be respected. I knew that my obsessions and compulsions still existed in some form. I resorted to them at times while working or reading. But the OCD was more tame than it had been. Eighteen-year-old me was content. I got my life back.

Insight: Counseling Portrayed

Counseling is unlike most other fields in that we rarely get to watch and observe professionals perform their work. Medical students shadow doctors, athletes watch sports, and actors go to the movies. Therapy is a more private profession for obvious reasons, but that makes it less observable. During an advanced techniques course in which we watched a counseling vignette, many students were quick to critique the example and the therapist's style from what we had learned — so much so that the professor was visibly and audibly defensive toward our feedback.

Fortunately for me, I had the opportunity to watch many therapists' styles in group and individual settings. I took what I liked and left what I didn't. At one internship site, I questioned the approaches of many of the therapists I shadowed since their techniques and styles varied greatly from what I was taught. When I did see a therapist whose style resonated with mine, I made sure to shadow her when I could. At another internship site, I was able to watch licensed professionals and valued the insight they offered in helping to process these sessions afterward.

Therapists who go to their own therapists are inevitably influenced by how those therapists work with them. While going to therapy is primarily for their own mental health, the therapist-patients get the added bonus of observing another therapist. In this way, their styles and philosophies are tied to their own therapists.

Faith and spirituality were closely tied to my first therapist as well as my current counselor. Both seamlessly incorporated faith in a helpful, kind, and nonjudgmental way rather than as an issue to shy away from. Their aims overall seemed to emphasize active listening and showing kindness rather than leaning on heavy analysis, despite my own overanalysis. That's not to say we did not explore deeper topics, such as my inner child, but it was more subtle.

My counselor Bill in particular has shown me the value of both self-disclosure and feedback. Sometimes when I would present an issue to him, instead of asking me a question or giving me guidance, he would tell a story. A few minutes later, a lightbulb would go off, and I'd realize how his story was what I needed to hear. Often, his sharing helped me put my problems in perspective, both validating me but also helping me to be realistic about my fears or concerns. As he would say, "Sometimes it's just not easy being Ross."

Work & OCD: Checked Out

An inconvenient workplace for a person with OCD is a library, a location where every book has a "right" place. My position was as a "page." I most often put away returned books and reorganized shelves, assisting with other tasks as needed. During my worst days, I'd reread titles of books and their authors over and over. Sometimes I'd hide while inserting and removing a book from its proper place if I hadn't thought about the "right" thing when I did so. This would occur in series of two or four but never three times, a phenomenon I couldn't explain.

Despite my mental health struggles, I was still good at my job and quite versatile, especially when finding a hard-to-track-down book or managing technical difficulties. My favorite task that served as respite from my monotonous duties was removing books that hadn't been checked out in a long time and fitting them into boxes for shipping. Then, too, did I reread titles and authors and insert and remove books from the boxes.

It was a year-and-a-half-long process to work on the overt OCD symptoms I experienced while balancing the challenges of school and work, but I began to find freedom. The library became a place of healing to practice my skills against OCD. When I began making progress, I could read a book without having to read the words "right," and it left me with an incredible feeling. When I didn't have to use compulsions at work, I enjoyed what I was doing far more.

There's a rush for being fearless, especially when I realized there was nothing to fear at all.

The Journey Continues

I became used to the routine schedule of studying or reading between classes, writing papers on Saturday mornings, and balancing homework with football on Sundays. My only breaks were for Wednesday night bowling and weekend nights when I would hang out with local friends. I was lonely, but I kept too busy to acknowledge this. School became my life.

I continued to work on my faith independently while managing my OCD tendencies. My junior year, I found myself at the university's club fair. I wandered from table to table and came across the Gamer's Club, which interested me from my years of gaming and my desire to find other "nerds" like me on campus. To my surprise, a charismatic student in his mid twenties flagged me over regarding the Men's Group, the college's religious group for male students. He was an aviation management major preparing to become a pilot. His talk was convincing, and I wrote down my name to get more information, debating if I would attend their first meeting.

This encounter changed the trajectory of both my college story and my life.

The first meeting of the Men's Group consisted of four young men squished together in the chaplain's office. It was far from ideal, and I considered leaving the group, but something compelled me to keep going. Not long after, we began meeting in larger conference rooms and having more profound discussion with more members attending. (In case you're wondering, I attended one meeting of the Gamer's Club and found I didn't belong.)

A semester later, I became a co-leader of the Men's Group, filling the empty spot of the student who had enlisted me and holding the position for three and a half years, running into my graduate years. I met many close friends and good men of faith through this group, some of whom still hold significance in my life.

There are certain interactions in life that would have changed everything if they hadn't happened. My meeting Dr. Shaw and his introduction to a more personal relationship with God is certainly one of them. The chance encounter with the aviation major is another, as it taught me that the simple act of reaching out can have radically important consequences. If he had chosen to sit on his phone or sulk about a lack of interest in his group that day, he may not have called me over or even noticed me. I might have walked by the table and missed an opportunity which would have changed the fabric of my life, from my friend group and living situations to, most importantly, my faith.

Chapter Five
My Near-Death Experience

5 Minutes Later

On the eve of Thanksgiving my senior year, I experienced my first near-death experience. It was an ordinary day. I had off from school for the holiday break, went for a haircut, and bowled in my Wednesday night bowling league. As I prepared to leave, my heart started racing, the result of a heart condition known as Wolff Parkinson White syndrome (WPW), which I presumably had from birth. It's an electrical issue with the heart that can cause a pre-excitation. In my case, there was an accessory pathway, and if the electrical signal went there, it wouldn't be regulated. This would cause my heart to race without the capability to slow down on its own, like a car going down a hill with no brakes. If my heart rate went to 160, 180, or 200 beats per minute and my heartbeat was irregular, it could cause serious problems, such as supraventricular tachycardia.

I was diagnosed with the condition at age 6 and started taking medication. I avoided caffeine in childhood for fear that it would make my heart race. I was discouraged from playing sports besides bowling. Still, I experienced an episode or two a year, during which I could usually slow down my heart rate through a variation of the Valsalva Maneuver. This required bringing my legs to my stomach with my arms and squeezing hard against my stomach. Sometimes when it didn't work, I would get nervous, but within a short time, it would slow down.

On this night, though, that didn't happen. My dad and I left the bowling alley, and I took more of my medication per the hospital's recommendations. They said that if my heartrate didn't slow down in an hour, I'd have to go to the emergency room for them to shock my heart back to a regular beat. An hour passed with no relief, so I went to the hospital. The staff started to give me medication through an IV. I vaguely remember seeing my heartrate drop. I think I saw a number in the 40s on the monitor before drifting off and hearing my mom yelling for me.

I woke up to find hospital staff, a doctor, and my parents circled around me with no idea how much time had passed. The doctor said that if I had come to the hospital even five minutes later, I would have been dead. I thanked God.

While I am grateful that they brought me back to life, to this day, I have doubts about what happened that night. I do not know if the hospital gave me the appropriate treatment to regulate my heart, or if it gave me the wrong medication. I later learned that as I laid in the hospital bed, staff members were aggressively questioning my mom outside about whether I was on drugs. She was yelling for me when I went into cardiac arrest, at which time the staff threw her out (they later let her back in the room in the hope that it would bring me back). They shocked me multiple times.

Reflection: Damar Hamlin

I had a missed call and an alarming text from my mom on the night of Jan. 2, 2023, when Damar Hamlin, a safety for the Buffalo Bills, collapsed on the field in Cincinnati after he went into cardiac arrest. When I called her back, she was audibly upset, reliving my hospital experience from a decade earlier, which gave me some new perspective on that night. Meanwhile, I could feel how physically rattled I was at hearing that someone on a global stage went into cardiac arrest. I never watched the replay; I couldn't bring myself to do that. It hit too close to home. I did, however, write a poem/reflection about Hamlin and the experience during the time he was unconscious when so many of us were checking our phones for any sign of good news. I called it "< 3" for the shape of a heart and his jersey number, 3.

Poem/Reflection: < 3

When tragedy strikes, it can't be helped but to look at ourselves. How we relate. How we might empathize with the victims and survivors. How we might picture our loved ones, their reactions to the pain. Sometimes, miles away, we can feel that heavy weight on our hearts — the stress headaches, tears that sting, nausea, cinder blocks for feet, hands frigid as if in a blizzard. Often we're unaware or desensitized to the trauma — no person can or should take this on. Our minds and bodies draw the line for us. But sometimes there is <u>that</u> tragic moment that seeps through, reminding us we are human. We are *fragile* despite our conviction that we have control. We can be hurt. Life isn't all fun, plans, and goals. In that tragic moment, we are shaken to remember this. <u>Yet</u>, I believe no suffering is meaningless. As we pray, help, and heal, may we find the purpose. May we keep hope and find that even in the worst of circumstances, our heart's intentions can be solidified for the better. And for those clinging on, give them healing or give them Heaven. I do not wish for anyone to die, but if you take one of my earthly neighbors, please let them end up in Your loving arms.

Hospital Week

Shortly after my near-death experience, I vomited on a medical staff member's shoes. I was embarrassed and felt so bad for him. I learned I bit my tongue while seizing during cardiac arrest. My mouth was dry from the medication, and they wouldn't let me drink water at the time. I was transported by ambulance from the local ER to the heart hospital 20 minutes south where my electrophysiologist was. There were talks about me being transferred by helicopter, but I ended up being stable enough for the ride.

I clonked out in the ambulance but remember waking up in the ICU to find two priests in the hallway. I don't know what denomination they were or why they were visiting at 11 o'clock the night before Thanksgiving, but they came over to my mom and me. They surrounded me and gave a blessing, perhaps the Anointing of the Sick. They gave my mom communion; I couldn't receive at that moment but still knew God was with me. The week or so I spent in that hospital I leaned on my faith. The words of a priest friend hold true, "We have as much faith as we need."

I spent a rollercoaster week in the hospital. On Thanksgiving, I was back to my usual self and must have been in total faith or complete denial about how I had nearly died, how my life was far more fragile, and how my future was far more uncertain than I could have imagined. I ate turkey and watched football. My family visited, and I was happy to see them, their Thanksgiving plans made irrelevant and replaced by gratitude that I was still there.

The next day, I went in for my first heart procedure, a catheterization, a simple treatment with a high success rate for those with WPW. Adele's "Skyfall" was playing on the radio as the staff prepped me and argued about what music my electrophysiologist wanted to listen to. I learned that the surgeon gets to pick the station.

In what might seem like an eerie experience, I partially woke up during the procedure, or what I thought was still the procedure, thinking I had to tell the surgeons about where my pain was and where to shock. You would think this would be scary, but I was somehow fine. I returned to my room, where I had to lay on my back for four hours. This was the most painful part of the procedure, as I was on a metal slab for a long period of time. This led to back pain for the next few weeks.

That night, my heart began to race. We learned the procedure had not been totally successful. My doctor monitored me hourly with the help of a nurse, who would call him to see if I should receive medication. My heart slowed by the morning, but it was an awful night. Imagine trying to sleep while your heart rate rests at 160 beats per minute. Somehow, though, I fell asleep.

It became apparent that another procedure was necessary. I went for a two-and-a-half-hour MRI that Monday, an event I actually looked forward to, as being in the hospital was one of the most boring experiences I've had.

A Usual Day as a Patient

On an average day in the hospital, I would be woken up at 4 in the morning for bloodwork — and by woken up, I mean that my door was opened to reveal the brightly burning fluorescent lights of the hallway. My groggy eyes opened to the reality that I was still in the dreaded hospital. The vampire, I mean phlebotomist, stated her intention to take my blood. A quick prick from a needle, and within 40 seconds, she was gone. Back to slumber I went.

Between the noises and lights, sleep was hard to come by in the hospital, especially between 11PM and midnight during third shift and at sunrise when the shift changed again and the nurses took vitals. Breakfast was served next, and then the debate began about whether I should shower, given the frequent discomfort of having an IV stuck in my arm and the seams of the canvas-like, green-blue hospital gown. The IV alone seemed to drain me by three energy levels. I would look out the window, wondering what the outside world was like. It felt as if I had been away for far longer than a few days. I went online here and there, but the internet was poor. I didn't have a smart phone in 2012, and cable TV didn't cut it for me either.

I walked the halls a few times a day, seeing some of the usual faces as well as some new ones among the patients and staff. I observed the visitors as they shuffled in to see loved ones. I requested the same rotation of two or three meals for lunch and dinner. The hospital burgers and grilled chicken were fantastic; I can still imagine how they tasted. My enthusiasm for either is somewhat dampened by the fact that they were hospital dishes.

Fortunately, I received so much love and support. Some friends visited, although I don't remember quite who. Many people checked up on me via messages, which put a lot of pressure on my brother to get back to them. God took care of me. God took care of us.

I went in for a second catheterization that Tuesday and left the hospital the day after, not cured of my issue but on medication to manage any future troubles I might have. I was happy to go home.

Can't Be the Same

Meanwhile, my fall semester was not yet over. My professors were kind and fair. One professor offered me an A if I did the final assignment, an A- if I didn't. Of course, I did the final assignment. Another professor said he would give me the notes and personally tutor me for one of the exams. I came into his office wearing a Holter monitor that I kept on for two weeks following my hospital stay and took the exam. I scored highest in the class. I ended that semester with a 4.0 GPA and then spent the winter break dead tired. I didn't get anyone a Christmas present. I was too exhausted. The only memory I have of that break is laying on my dad's recliner, watching an America concert with my parents.

From there, my academic lifestyle began to change. How could it not? For so long, I had made school my main focus, but there was so much more to life. I no longer wanted to work as hard at academics as I once did. Rather, I prioritized spending time with friends.

I decided to live in such a way that if that day was my last, I would have enjoyed how I spent it.

The traumatic but inspiring event of my near-death experience sparked intentionality. However, it also brought with it an unnecessary sense of urgency I wouldn't recognize for years. Feeling as if you're encouraged to take risks in life can be freeing, yet being pushed to make certain decisions right away for that you'll miss your chance? Well, it's not an ideal way to think, even if that day is your last. I can attest that this mindset has contributed to obsessiveness and rushing in terms of dating, finances, seeking independence, and meeting expectations. There are days where it does not feel like there is enough time.

For graduate school, I applied to my university's school psychology program, which was known for being small and selective. I sat alone in my living room and opened the acceptance letter.

I had been accepted. I became one of four members of my cohort, which included one of my best friends, whom I considered a sister. This was the very program that my mother and I had investigated when I was still in high school. Back then, the advisers had chuckled that I had started my grad school search so early. Well, I made it. I immediately started crying. I didn't know why. Yet I knew they were not happy tears. Something was not right.

I graduated cum laude from my undergraduate program and started graduate school a few days later. Technically, I had already started taking graduate courses as an undergrad, but this would be official. I knew I would miss my undergraduate friends dearly over the summer, as I often did until some of them stayed local. My high school friends were no longer in my life for reasons I still don't understand.

I found out not long before the semester that I received a graduate assistantship, working for the physician's assistant program and the Office of Outcomes and Assessment. It paid for nine credits per semester and also included a meager stipend, which was sufficient for me since I still lived at home. I wrapped up work as a research assistant to one of my favorite professors, a job I enjoyed as I learned about the importance of social capital, the concept that connections are valuable for the opportunities and resources they can offer. As the old adage goes, it's not what you know, it's who you know. I've found through life how valuable our connections are.

Chapter Six
Grad School
My True College Experience

Same Place But Different

During graduate school, I was much more involved on campus. It felt like the undergraduate experience I didn't get to have. Truly, Marywood University became my second home. I would go to work at the graduate assistantship in the morning, come home for a few hours, come back for a night class, then attend a religious group or see what friends were around. Some nights I'd even wander the campus, not sure what I was looking for, yet hoping something magical might happen.

I became more focused on friendships and dating than academics, as I had fewer classes to manage and found them to be far easier than I expected. Classes repeated a lot of content from their undergraduate counterparts but with less seasoned professors and less challenging material.

I also felt resistance toward my school psychology program. I typically didn't want to be involved in program events. I extended how long the school psychology program was, not wanting to overwhelm myself with twelve-credit semesters and no summers off. I didn't even know the names of my classes, referring to them instead by their shortened names from the course catalog.

Yet, I glimpsed my growing passion to counsel others. I entered the school psychology program initially intending to counsel high school students. I wanted to help teenagers who didn't feel like they belonged in school or weren't reaching their full potential.

The Sparks for Counseling

A meaningful nudge toward the counseling field came in my first week of graduate school while working as a graduate assistant for the physician's assistant program. The previous year, a student died by suicide, which left those in the program heartbroken. The program director wanted more information on college counseling centers to compare other colleges' centers to Marywood's. What began as a task to heal the program and help struggling students resulted in my professional contribution — a project to complete my graduate studies — which I named "Mental Health on College Campuses: Need for Policy and Guidelines." I wish that this paper made more impact than collecting dust on my shelf, but maybe it helped my adviser feel as if we were making a difference out of a tragic event. When someone takes their own life, there tends to be no resolution. There is no remedy. I truly hope I helped the program director with my work.

Meanwhile, I found my love for counseling through the one counseling class we took in the school psychology program. I heeded every word of this class. I was engrossed in how my professor presented the basic counseling skills, similar to how Daniel LaRusso in the *Karate Kid* secretly learned karate through chores assigned by Mr. Miyagi. As Daniel completed each task in the hot sun, frustrated that he was no closer to learning karate, a challenge by his wise sensei showed him that each of those seemingly unrelated movements came together to form the foundation of defending himself. Likewise, my learning how to ask open-ended questions and use paraphrasing led to holding cohesive mock therapy sessions. I wanted to learn more. The meticulous transcribing of my mock sessions and hearing my professor's feedback felt meaningful. This was a field I could work in.

For so long, I fought what my school psychology classes were teaching me. An adjunct professor's transparency about his work was instrumental in discovering that I wanted to leave the school psychology program. I hoped that more of my job description could be counseling instead of conducting early assessments on children, writing individualized education programs (IEPs), and holding meetings with parents and staff. I could not picture myself giving assessments to kids or sitting alone in a closet-sized office at a school. I shunned the thought of having to cater to each parent's whims. Attending meetings and generating IEPs that I could not guarantee would be effectively executed sounded dreadful. I was passionate about education reform, but not about being a school psychologist.

The final, convincing push came at a retreat in my second year of graduate school. I was part of Big House, an on-campus Christian group known for its co-ed hallway and notoriously looked down upon as a cult. I was already leader of the Men's Group and attended Bible Study and adoration. Most of my friends were in these groups or 4:12 for Women, the university's Christian women's group, so becoming a part of Big House was an easy decision, even as a commuter.

Each semester Big House had a retreat. Retreats can be a faith-filled time of deep reflection, relaxation, catharsis, and growth, especially when surrounded by trusted friends. Over that weekend, I saw close friends break down about their personal issues, stirring a desire to be there for them in their struggle. Processing this experience with a trusted friend that week led me to make the change in my studies.

Fortunately, my university had a program in place that offered the counseling classes I would need for the state's counseling license without having to pursue another master's degree. My parents questioned the decision, as school psychology felt like the more lucrative and safe option, yet they were somehow convinced to trust my decision.

I was accepted into the program and would have nine credits a semester paid for through my graduate assistantship. God was certainly taking care of me.

What Happened on the Dance Floor

About a year after my breakup with my first girlfriend, I met a woman who enamored me with her beauty and sparked me with her creativity. She was spontaneous, affectionate, and free-spirited. As a relatively contained, play-it-safe kind of individual, she drew me in. She danced in the rain; I took cover.

We met at College Dance Night, the ballroom dancing event a friend and I organized to offer college students the opportunity for a sober hangout away from the bars. She and I clicked on the dance floor.

Initially, I basked in the excitement of receiving the kind of attention I had not received before. However, the early sparks of dating began to fade as inconveniences and difficult situations became more commonplace. She struggled personally, which led to issues within the relationship. Her schedule became so packed with schoolwork and work that we rarely had time to develop hobbies or spend much quality time together. Meanwhile, I began to feel my boundaries becoming obscured.

I was fairly inexperienced with relationships, having had just one serious adult relationship prior to her entering my life. Her flirting and questions often made me feel uncomfortable, which says far more about my lack of dating than about her. My Catholic guilt and lack of exposure to romance and intimacy made me feel like a prude. I struggled both morally and relationally. My lack of experience and heavy boundaries proved to be barriers and high levels of discomfort.

I noticed that I was distancing myself from God during this time, spending less time at adoration on Wednesday nights and pushing Him aside when I was focused on my romantic relationship. I was disconnecting from Him. The relationship with her also created an imbalance in my family, as I stayed out later and spent more time away from home. I felt a greater urge to separate from my parents with my girlfriend as my motivation.

Letting Her Go

Given some difficult situations we endured together and those that put me between a rock and a hard place with her and my family, I opted to end the relationship early in my counseling program. Yet, I wanted to help her more. I had felt like her only true support. Leaving her almost felt like abandoning her with her struggles. The conclusion that I could do little for her presented inner conflict, knowing I had to set boundaries instead of remaining by her side.

In distancing myself from her, I experienced situations in which I questioned my stance. I identified as a helper, but I couldn't help her, or I could help her but chose not to — was I a horrible person? I did not want to insert myself into a situation with her knowing that I would not be able to stay and be a stable part of her support system long-term.

I felt deep loneliness and shame. There were aspects about her I felt I couldn't tell my family or friends out of respect for her privacy, similarly how I am not sharing these details in this book. My breakup with her led me back to seeing a counselor, my first counseling experience since my freshman-year sessions with Dr. Shaw.

On a Friday morning, I walked from my graduate assistantship to the counseling center, where I would start sessions with two doctoral students from the psychology doctoral program. I had been crying in an office by myself while texting my best friend. I knew I couldn't handle the breakup by myself.

Considering the mix of feelings I experienced, I didn't get a chance to process actually missing her and the good times we had together for quite some time, even with counseling. The guilt and shame I felt when recollecting my experience with her often came out as resentment. This happened in the initial drafts of this very book. The justified anger I felt toward her seemed to defend my position that I was a victim. However, in gaining feedback for this book, I realized that holding grudges toward her for self-protection was unhealthy on my part. Instead, it was better to accept the situation for what it was and let the details float away on the wind.

Chapter Seven
My First Counseling Experiences

First Opportunity

I loved my new counseling classes. I soaked up information like a sponge. I hadn't even stepped foot in an actual counseling session besides my own, but I wanted to be involved. Graduating with my master's degree in psychology and starting my new counseling program was the recharge I needed.

My practicum, a 100-hour clinical experience, was to take place at a nearby college. It was my mother's alma mater, and I had walked by there numerous times as a child while going to the local libraries. Two counseling friends and I were initially promised an opportunity to train in a new counseling center the school had developed, but what we got was a skills-based program for students who got in trouble. As punishment for their offenses, they received psychoeducation about life skills, such as healthy communication, from me and my fellow interns. Fortunately, we were able to use our counseling skills in listening to students who truly needed empathy.

I heard stories of institutional racism and drug use while there. We did outreach programs on mental health and sexual consent. Getting enough clinical hours with students to meet the practicum requirements was difficult since it was a small college and not many students came to us for sessions. To make up for that, I volunteered to counsel students at my university in a program separate from the counseling center and to give talks to freshmen boys about sexual consent.

Will Work for Free

My next step was to find an internship site. I applied for about 10 internship positions, but many places were not accepting interns. One private practitioner met with me, explaining how I could even make money as his intern, but he later ghosted me when I needed more information. With the semester quickly approaching, I entered his office unannounced to find that he, like many others, couldn't take me on. I struggled to understand why I kept hitting wall after wall.

Enraged, I began walking to a Jewish counseling center a few blocks away. No resumé in hand, only me, determined for my chance. It would have been a great story if my boldness won me an internship opportunity, but unfortunately they, too, were not taking interns. You would think more people would have wanted free labor. (Today, I would be booked immediately if I offered free sessions.)

My college group supervisor helped me connect with Kristy, a licensed professional counselor (LPC) and certified rehabilitation counselor (CRC) who had recently joined a group practice. I wanted to learn about the private-practice world. The next day, I also received a call from a drug and alcohol facility known as Humble Beginnings Counseling (HBC). After an interview, I got in and went from having zero internships to two in less than a week.

The following semester, I reduced my hours at the drug and alcohol internship, which was risky, but pursued hours at my college's counseling center, the very place where I got my personal introduction to the counseling experience, sitting in "that chair." It was also where I was receiving post-breakup services at the time. With three internship positions, it was the most well-rounded internship experience I could have asked for.

Insight: Counselor Education

I've often heard clients accuse therapists of their learning coming from books. This was meant as an insult, insinuating a lack of understanding or life experience. A significant piece of my early counseling knowledge and skills came from mentors, training, and unsurprisingly, my clients. Much of what I learned in graduate school was active listening skills and ethical considerations. I also learned the basics about effective modalities, such as cognitive behavioral therapy. The focus from my education was person-centered, a style focused on validating the client with authenticity — an unconditional, positive regard and no judgment. This is common-sense therapy. I view it as "the improv of counseling" since it uses the least script and offers the most room to play. Its principles shape the session significantly. While being person-centered makes a therapist flexible, it lacks interventions.

I had the foundation I needed when I left my counseling program; however, there was much more to learn. I didn't know how to write a progress note or maintain proper documentation. I wasn't aware of how to start my own practice, bill insurance, or manage the financial responsibilities of self-employment. Truly, I would have wanted more focus put onto these areas. Additionally, I would have benefitted from more exposure to interventions and specialties. I would have preferred to see more professor demonstrations rather than learn the concepts from books or presentations.

What many clients do not realize is that I learned much of my clinical and business skills on the go. Clinically, most of the interventions and philosophies I use come from my own work regarding OCD, my faith, and headaches. Consuming therapy media, talking to colleagues, and experiencing my own therapy are among my greatest sources of learning. Business-wise, my colleague Kristy taught me the most about running my private practice. My financial adviser, accountant, and Facebook groups helped in significant ways, too.

Learning a New Way

Personally at this time, I was dealing with the aftermath of my last relationship and continued my own counseling. My close friendships deepened as many of my friends who graduated with me lived locally. I was living at home, which would become more cramped as four grown adults often shared three rooms. I had fallen out of my faith to an extent and would soon learn how to live my faith in different ways as I confronted some important questions with God about relationships and where I belonged in the church.

I completed my three internships and my counseling program. I embarked on my journey as a pre-licensed professional therapist.

Chapter Eight
Humble Beginnings Counseling (HBC)

Hole-in-the-Wall Agency

I began working about ten minutes after handing in the completion paperwork for the LPC program at Marywood University. My first job was at Humble Beginnings Counseling (HBC), where I had interned and spent six months shadowing groups and evening running some of my own.

During my first group session there as an intern, I sat awkwardly in a polo and khakis as my facilitator forgot to introduce me. I was nervous and found myself ruminating on the ethics of observing the group unannounced. I followed the facilitator, realizing his tone was much harsher than mine and his questioning more aggressive than I had learned in my training. An hour in, my facilitator finally introduced me.

At one point, a client commented that I didn't look like an addict. I was taken aback and oddly offended. In a strange way, I wanted to belong. It was true, though — I was not an addict. I hadn't seen drugs like marijuana, cocaine, or heroin, let alone taken any of them. I grew up with alcohol casually left on kitchen counters, nothing special about it. The friends I once had who got into drinking were no longer my friends. Frankly, there was a lot more I needed to learn about this field and about myself.

MISTER ROSS

I earned $14 an hour part-time to run four three-hour-long groups. Sometimes a few members showed; other times, the group was unreasonably large. I made an agreement with the owner to stay for six months. The best way I can depict my experience at HBC was through a poem I wrote and adapted:

Alan Alda, famously known as Benjamin "Hawkeye" Pierce on the legendary show M*A*S*H*, coined the phrase "meatball surgery" to describe the medical marvels the 4077 performed in the operating room on the grounds of a mobile Army surgical hospital. Sutures were done quickly and efficiently so as to save necessary resources and the next person-in-line's life under the many constraints of their war-torn environment. In my feeble attempt to compare my work to that of this high fictional status, I have coined the counseling I did at my first job as "meatball counseling."

A whiff of smoke hits me in the face as I open the door to the facility. I head up the steps, carpeted and covered in stains, the wallpaper peeling, colored a forgettable beige or gray or puke green. The first left brings me to the waiting room. Cheap, older couches and, once again, stains. There is a theme here. A prominent wooden display of the agency's logo hangs next to a plaque for best internship site from a local college. Clients squeeze in one by one, some from halfway houses, others yet to be sentenced in the wild west of the county court system, and others who signed their rights away through treatment court. Some make jokes or sit in awkward silence, awaiting their facilitator in the smaller group room.

They are from all walks of life. From teens and twenty-somethings, practically babies, to "old heads," from the wise and open to learn about themselves to the skeptic who seeks long-winded stories over self-discovery, or the quiet to not be stirred, who fully intends to use substances once their oversight is gone.

Group is about to begin. It is at this point that the fluorescent light-filled squares, duct tape on the floor, cheap metal chairs hard against your bottom, and ugly third-class artwork is morphed into a haven of safety, a community of understanding. The transformation is incredible; the chaos fades away. A group of strangers support one another. Though the two are seemingly different, here they are quite similar.

Members relate with the common bond of addiction, but their ties run deeper. They feel loss, desire validation, face conflict, and avoid hardship in ways that are common. They fear uncertainty, show frustration, apologize for their tears, and mask their upset with "content." They refer to the non-addict as normal and regular people, out there and on the streets. They do not realize how normal they are but how their worlds are not.

Their world, centered in my mind at this counseling agency, is truly across our cities and our globe. But I had contained addiction to this place, where the smoke is thick and the problem is distanced from my childhood, geriatric Italian community. But this is naïve. They are truly we.

The conversation grows deeper for some. A-ha moments are apparent, disclosures are shared; meanwhile, others stare blankly at the floor or at the inside of their eyelids, nodding off from another relapse. Not all choose to join in the group, though all are welcome. As the finish of the three-hour group draws near, members are on the edge of their seats to rejoin the world that has filled them with destruction. Some run for the door, while others linger to offer support or have a court-ordered AA sheet signed to appease the judge. Now the room is back to a mess.

I return to my office, three desks scattered about a grayed, once-pink carpet beneath my feet. I sit down in a green chair, duct tape wrapped around the arms, at a desk just my size, a vent above my head black as soot pouring the cool AC upon my hair and cardigan. I'm filled with hope as I look to my bulletin board where I have pinned my feeling sheet, a five-chapter poem about change which fits on an 8.5" by 11," and three tiny slips of hole-punched paper taped to the board I found the morning when I prayed for God's intervention — they had formed two eyes and a smiling mouth. Even in this place, God was with me, and only by the Holy Spirit can a horrid room filled with total strangers in terrible situations produce a therapeutic experience. I see in their hearts they want to be in this place. They've built a community here, understanding, validation, a sense of comradery, and shared struggle. They get what they need, which is the goal of therapy, but the counselor needs to get what they need as well.

So when I say "meatball counseling," this is what I mean. We seek to get through today, or this hour, or this minute, one day at a time. All in an effort to make this day a little better than the last. "Meatball counseling" is truly fostering hope and growth in a dead place. In this way, seeds are planted to flower from the bricks and the ashes.

Transition from College

This time in my life was a slow transition from college to the workforce. I had a fairly easy schedule with three days off, which was necessary to cope with how stressful work was. I had stopped my own personal counseling for a time- and began dating more often. When asked, "How's the girl?" I would sometimes not know what girl they were referring to. I wasn't by any means a stud, and while I teased I was a player, I was far from it. I kept learning that the women I was dating weren't for me.

I was 25, still living at home, sharing a small room and a bunk bed with my brother. We'd play video games until late., which wasn't the best for our relationship or my sleep schedule. I had no privacy. I love my family, but I don't know how we managed to live under the same roof together for that long. Yet, I didn't have the money or the thought process to seriously consider moving out.

Friend-wise, I had my group of Catholic friends from Marywood as well as my counselor friends from a previous internship. Sometimes I'd have the two groups come together for hangouts. On one such occasion at a local bar/restaurant, we enjoyed drinks together at a table. Tipsy off one drink, I stumbled to the bathroom. Meanwhile, they colluded against me and switched tables without my knowing. I came back to the table and informed them that my chair felt wobbly. They casually played my comment off. About 20 minutes later, I realized they had changed tables on me to their laughter. They got me.

I was learning how to be a counselor and an adult. I had minimal independence, a great group of friends, no significant other, yet plenty of anger. Working at my agency fueled me. I realized early on in my career what I didn't want from a workplace and ways I wouldn't run my own counseling business.

Insight: Not Far Off

I found it incredible how I related to my clients. Despite their addiction to substances or serious mental health issues, I discovered common threads. Sometimes I felt I could relate more to them because in a sense I was an outsider like them. I grew up an outsider — I was bullied, I had different hobbies, most of the time I kept to myself, and it wasn't until college that I found a group of like-minded people. However, I can easily pick out shared experiences and feelings.

Themes resonate loudly in counseling — not feeling one is worthwhile or loveable, that the same cycle will repeat itself no matter how hard the person tries, and that people cannot be trusted. You and I can relate to all of those. Sure, the contexts and severity of these issues may vary. For some, these are passing thoughts or late-night moments, while for others they are core beliefs and rigid ideologies, some written in stone and others invisible to the untrained eye.

Another aspect of counseling that I've concluded is divine intervention is that clients often share issues that resonate with areas of my life, sometimes lessons that I learned even days previously. The resemblance is spooky. Usually, I feel a sense of gratitude that I went through the situation to help my client. Other times I'm in awe at the lesson I learned or the next piece of the puzzle I needed along my own journey. Of course, I bring the attention back to my client, but I also have the wisdom I need to grow. One of the hidden benefits of being a therapist is that you gain more opportunity to grow by hearing about the growth of others and helping them with their growth.

Not All Bad

The interactions in groups during that first job were sometimes so out of control I could barely speak. This assignment felt out of my league from the beginning, yet my clients accepted me and listened when I did share. I grew in confidence during my time there in large part to a mentor who showed me the ropes. She challenged me to think outside the box for group therapy and to put deep caring for clients into action. She encouraged me to speak in groups and took my feedback even though she was far more seasoned than I was.

Meanwhile, I gained the respect of a cranky supervisor through my football knowledge and standing my ground. However, I took this pursuit so seriously that it was comical. This supervisor was not shy about saying inappropriate things about clients, which made me angry. When I would correct him, I sensed he respected me. On one occasion, he said something about a "yellow" client, to which I immediately rebutted that the term was "Asian American," as if I was reciting one of Walter's lines from *The Big Lebowski*. He burst out laughing and went to a coworker, sharing that he meant yellow as in jaundice. This yellow tone of the skin can occur among needle users and alcoholics because of liver issues. That one was on me. I'm proud of myself for being so bold to stand up to him, even when common sense should have told me his statement was benign.

This job also gave me my first work nickname, "The Machine." Two of my supervisors teased me for my initiative, one stating that no intern had ever asked him for more work. But I desperately wanted to learn more about counseling. I was an eager, bright-eyed intern turned novice. Being in college for seven and a half years, I truly wanted to start helping others and soak in what counseling had to offer right away.

My group work there especially felt fulfilling. Some clients sought out my groups in particular, which was validating. I had to approach counseling authentically. I couldn't fake caring. The stories I heard could have beat out any TV show drama or blockbuster hit. I was compelled to listen.

Insight: Self-Disclosure

I have found it important to use self-disclosure from time to time. Some clients ask me questions about myself, from basics like how old I am (because I look younger than my age) to more complex topics, like how I might handle a situation. On one occasion, a client asked me what it was like for me to be in the group with them, which required a thoughtful and honest response. For the purpose of connection and transparency, I like to give an answer as opposed to pushing the question back to the client or asking why they asked me; counselors delaying their genuine answers with extra questions can deter connection. I took this guidance from Irvin Yalom, and it's been positive for me. As he discusses in *The Gift of Therapy*, clients will return to talking about themselves once we counselors self-disclose. They won't stay too long on details about us. I've found this to be true.

Admittedly, I've at times felt uncomfortable with the little admissions I've made with clients but have chosen to share when appropriate. For example, when clients tell me they don't value their birthday, sometimes this leads into work on self-worth and a story about one of my birthdays. On one birthday in particular, I didn't have a party but instead went to a bar with a friend where someone else's birthday was being celebrated. I didn't know the majority of people there, including the person whose birthday it was. I felt alone, forgotten, and foolish for going. I decided that on my next birthday, I would treat myself better. Each birthday since, I've held a party to celebrate, even if it was combined with others. I still felt seen and valued, even if I didn't feel worthy. On another birthday not long after the one in that first story, I took myself out for the day for shopping and lunch. Telling a story like this can show that I'm human, too. I didn't have all the answers and doubted myself. However, I made a bold change based on not wanting to feel the way I did.

HBC Family

My boss at the initial job interview asked if I was in recovery, which is both an inappropriate yet common question in the drug and alcohol field. I was not, which was the disadvantage I worked against during much of my time there. Yet, at this moment, it was an advantage. My boss responded that too many addicts made for a "sick family." Every one of the therapists and supervisors there was in recovery; I was the only one who was not. I learned more from them and their stories than I could have from a course or book.

I liked some but not all of the people I worked with. I chatted with one guy about football and his kids. A younger woman and I talked about our love lives, sang Justin Bieber songs on a Friday afternoon, and on one occasion, went to the movies, during which she shouted to the whole theater that I was crying during *Christopher Robin*. I visited a supervisor's church a couple times for praise and worship nights. A middle-aged female coworker kissed me on the cheek once and flirted with me, enough to make me a tad uncomfortable yet validate me.

The most telling story of my work environment was when a coworker with a personal story of recovery, an undergraduate degree, and a chip on her shoulder joined our staff. I've worked with therapists before who had an aura of arrogance about them but the knowledge and expertise to back it up. This therapist did not. She often cut off my suggestions when I shadowed her groups as an intern.

She was cocky even with the clients. During one group session, she got into a heated debate with a client from a halfway house. This is one of the few times in a session that I legitimately thought a client might attack a facilitator. The clinical director overheard the conversation from his office and proceeded to walk into the group room and lay down in the middle of the floor, moving the room from seething tension to confusion to laughter. He said a few words and left.

Following the group, I voiced frustration to my mentor about this unprofessional intervention, but looking back, his redirection, while uncanny, was genius. He defused an entire group and prevented what could have been a serious incident with significant consequences. The therapist soon after transferred to another facility with fewer clients.

Overall, between the boss and clinical director yelling at each other or various coworkers, tense staff meetings, the poor condition of the office, under-qualified therapists, and strange workplace dynamics, this was the most dysfunctional work environment I have ever been part of. Back then it was depressing; now it's comical and depressing. However, being there was an incredible learning experience I wouldn't trade for anything. God had clearly led me there for a season. With the help of a friend setting me up with an interview at a nearby drug and alcohol facility, I left mere days over the agreed upon six-month mark.

Ultimately, we helped clients. And that's what a therapist does. When I once complained in a group practice consultation about therapists who lacked training, a wise social worker responded saying that the therapist's qualifications do not matter if they're helping someone. While I still advocate for proper training, ethics, and gatekeeping in the field, I cannot say she was wrong.

Insight: "Reconciling Takes Two, Forgiveness Takes One"

We cannot gain closure directly from another person. Instead, closure comes from a choice we make to forgive or let go of another person. We can certainly reconnect with someone who hurt us, and even grow from the experience, but this is not necessary for letting go of resentment and bitterness. Forgiveness is the act of letting go of negative feelings toward another, thereby freeing ourselves. Resentments hurt us, not the other person. Forgiveness heals us, not the other person. It is not our responsibility to heal another for how they hurt us. We can reconcile with them and ensure the relationship is better, but that usually means letting go of the hurts we've suffered. Sometimes our resentments tie in with our beliefs, resentments toward others, and even criticism we have toward ourselves. A healthy level of forgiving on our own and bringing God into a relationship for His spiritual healing are key.

Insight: Guardedness

Early on, one of my biggest struggles was learning that not every client wants help. I wanted so badly to help people — to learn about their stories, to engage in the counseling process, and to walk through therapy together. Well, that's not always how it goes. In fact, I learned it was rare that someone wanted my help at drug and alcohol facilities. Most of the clients were court-mandated or encouraged to attend for legal reasons. That being said, many clients didn't want counseling, didn't understand why they were there, or didn't know what counseling was. I often felt pushed away or rejected by clients. Often, I'd see a lack of participation, attempts to monopolize the counseling process, or repetitive and unproductive complaining. But what I would come to find was that this was the part of the counseling process I loved — helping clients work through their initial guardedness or "resistance" to the process.

The majority of my work in the drug and alcohol world involved talking about therapy and wellness/sobriety. We wouldn't jump right into how to make changes but rather focused on what the changes might look like or if they would be beneficial. Many clients walk into therapy with barriers. They might not believe in counseling. They might be frustrated with their legal charges and the system. They may hesitate to share their problems or be vulnerable with another person. They may not trust anyone.

Consider the "contemplative" stage of change, when people discuss and think about making a change but aren't at the point of planning or making it. Every person comes into therapy with some barrier to their goals; otherwise, they would have accomplished them already. Furthermore, people are logical and autonomous. They aren't going to put work into something that they aren't comfortable enough with or that they don't think is worth their time. Counselors need to be patient and build relationships with their clients. People participating in therapy need to be patient with themselves and open to change, even when it's uncomfortable or novel. The therapeutic relationship maintains this balance.

Dusting the Dirt from My Feet: Leaving HBC

Here is an adapted journal excerpt about me leaving HBC:

Everyone had already left the building. It was 2PM, and my last Saturday-morning group had finished. I learned to hate this place over these past six months. The smell, the walls, the carpets, the chairs. I hated the greed, what it stood for, the person who owned it. It was an emotional group for me, and I was compelled to sit at the top of the steps and linger for a moment. As I tuned into my feelings, I began to tear up, realizing that goodbyes were said and this was my last Saturday group, my pride and joy at HBC. At first I was adamant about not working weekends, but I am glad I opened up to the idea. So I did what I did when I finished my last counseling session with a counselor in December — I sat with it. The feelings, the goodbyes, the transition to a new chapter of my life. And for the first time in this place, I felt at peace, accepting where my journey brought me and where it would take me next.

A few minutes passed, and I knew it was time to go. I reached acceptance of what was. No intentions to go back, no intentions to stay, no regrets about the way I ran groups or leaving this place or who I was. I came into this field as a person looking to help people. At first, I had no idea how to help those in my groups or on my caseload. What I was told later was that the most important things were that I listened, I didn't push my agenda on others, I was patient, I did my best to understand, and I could relate outside the boundaries of addiction. When I was preparing to leave, I didn't understand my impact on those I worked with, but later learned that **who I am is as important to my work as what I do.** I walked down the stairs, locked the door, and remembered I needed to return my key. I debated playing music on the way home but decided to sit with this feeling for a little while longer.

Insight: Client Buy-In

What I learned was that people would buy into me, and groups would buy into the culture of the group. With my unhappy mandated clients, I had to find the careful balance of understanding and, in some cases, agreement, along with the delicate approach of addressing the issues — why the person was here and what they could gain.

Groups became a joy, both participating in and witnessing the process. If I could get one group to take ownership despite their guardedness to be there, new members would see this and want to be part of it, too. There were bumps in the road, of course. Members leaving and group dynamics changing were jarring at times. But for the most part, people bought in, and that was satisfying as a facilitator.

Learning how to meet people where they were has been helpful for two reasons. One, I learned a skill they could only scratch the surface of in college.

There are so many unique individuals who walk into treatment with their stories, situations, and reasons for being there. It would be impossible to map out how to handle guardedness in many of these cases. However, the process of working with a person where they are has become instinctual. Two, I learned that I don't need the validation of my clients in order to do my job effectively. I could be as passionate and enthusiastic about what I share regardless if they're invested. Hopefully in time they are.

In private-practice settings, people are typically less guarded, more receptive, and there voluntarily. Many of my clients sought me through previous facilities, *Psychology Today*, an online database for prospective clients to view profiles of therapists, and trusted referral sources. I'm honored when someone chooses me to be their counselor. When a client is referred to me by a colleague who trusted me enough to do so, I feel validated.

The skills I learned with mandated clients who didn't want counseling help me significantly now. Court-mandated or not, people may have trouble trusting someone new. We all have our defenses. Some people distract with less important issues, others minimize, and others ramble. Some people cancel frequently or don't do their homework. The tactics are fascinating. As trust is being built, I could call out individuals for these behaviors and work to have a more honest approach to counseling. Their openness to feedback and willingness to respond in healthier ways is, in and of itself, therapeutic progress.

Chapter Nine
Moving Forward & Faith
Intentional Treatment Counseling (ITC)

Starting Out

I embarked on two and a half years at a new drug and alcohol agency, Intentional Treatment Counseling (ITC), a place I both loved and hated. Initially, I felt I had made it. ITC was regarded as the top outpatient drug and alcohol facility in the area. However, it also was viewed with animosity by a familiar competitor, my previous workplace, for its connections to the court system. In every way, ITC outperformed where I came from — the environment, the clinical expertise and education, the management, technology, documentation, the weekly staff meeting, the offices, and the group rooms.

My interview was relaxed. The CEO played music as he and his second in command, a supervisor, asked me questions and laughed with me for an hour. I was told that my references were the best ones the supervisor had ever received. I was honest about my future plans during the interview, knowing I wasn't going to stay in the drug and alcohol field for my entire career. What struck me as the CEO gave me a tour of the building was his frustration with a stain on the carpet of a group room. I was relieved that this place would be different, knowing that they cared about the therapeutic environment as much as I did.

I started work the week of my birthday in June 2017. I was asked after my first staff meeting when my birthday was, to which I shyly responded that it was that day. Two of the supervisors sang "Happy Birthday" to me on the spot. I had my own office and, not long after, a plaque with my name on the door. The men wore ties and slacks. This place was official.

However, in time I found that much of the nice features, which remained vast improvements from my last agency, were a façade. There was frequent gossip and rumors. The paperwork was intense. While I believed my coworkers supported me, I did not feel the company itself had my back.

Many employees struggled with the issues I noticed. I did, too, but I'd sometimes laugh to myself that they had no idea how bad things could be. This place was a tropical island compared to my previous workplace.

Falling in Faith

I was missing the sense of belonging and accountability as I practiced my faith more by myself. To voice my struggles in a meaningful way, I volunteered to give a talk at an XLT event in Stroudsburg, Pennsylvania. XLT, short for Exalt, are church events centered around worshiping God through prayer, scripture, music, confession, and fellowship. Often, a young person gives a speech, a priest reads the Gospel and offers a homily, live music is played, and priests and nuns would attend. This was the place to meet fellow Catholics.

I loved these events, especially those that occurred on a Friday night, as a way to relax after the week and prioritize God. Meanwhile, I experienced the bonus of spending time with my friends and having free desserts, which also meant taking home the leftover cookies.

Putting One's Faith Into Action

My talk was on the importance of being transparent about our struggles while living out our faith, titled "Putting One's Faith Into Action", an adapted version here:

I'd like to start this talk with a quote from Cardinal Suhard: "Live in such a way that one's life would not make sense if God did not exist."

Amazing, right? That's the goal, the ideal. But we don't always meet that. By a show of hands, who here is brave enough to say that at one point or another, even as recently as this week, you have struggled with your faith?

I'm here to say that's normal.

For me, I remember as a grad student, I was no longer involved with religious groups on-campus. I was a leader of Men's Group for three and a half years, a member of Big House Christian Living, and a weekly participant at Bible study and adoration. I was sitting on a bench in the fall realizing I wasn't happy with my faith. That same feeling perpetuated beyond that moment, and my faith remained stagnant as long as I didn't do anything with that feeling. A simple and profound message I heard during a faith-based talk sums it up — "If you do something, something will happen. If you do nothing, nothing will happen."

Sometimes we become stagnant in our relationship with God for a number of reasons — it's not so simple. While we each have a story, there is a common thread to all of our stories. We've all had our "20 seconds of insane courage," so to speak, but we've had our low points in faith, too. Reflect with me for a moment. How about the times where everything was good? We got the grade we wanted or the job we dreamt of, the relationship we hoped for... and so we put God to the side. Or maybe we were feeling "content" with life. Nothing too good or bad, yet we forget that God makes the ordinary extraordinary. But what about when life knocks us down? Those times when we lost someone who was important to us, or we felt like we'd have one inconvenience after the other, or we were hurt and it wasn't fair. That God wasn't listening or didn't care. I can relate. I've lost hope before, and honestly, I'm only starting to get it back now. In the two and a half months leading up to this talk, I can say I've been struggling with my faith, to the point that I didn't feel worthy to be up here in front of you. I felt lost until I started to hear little by little people struggled with their faith, too. It wasn't just me. For those of you who are struggling with your faith tonight or aren't quite making God your No. 1 priority in life on a consistent basis, you're not alone; I'm with ya. That's why I feel I am meant to be here giving this talk.

As humans, we struggle to reach that pinnacle of being witnesses to God. We often forget what is best for us. We sin because we lose sight of what's important, because we don't get why God wants us to do this or avoid that, because we lose hope in His plan for us. We grab the reins of the wild horse called life and say that we got this, but alone we find ourselves thrown off that horse again and again.

All that may sound negative and defeating, but bear with me because that's not where this ends because we are born for so much more — it's gonna take some work, but it's also gonna take some hope. God sees us for how we can be, not simply as we are now. During confession at an XLT event, the priest in persona Christi said, "God loves you, God forgives you, and there is hope." Let me say that again. "God loves you, God forgives you, and there is hope." Personally, I cling to those words and set a reminder on my phone to see them everyday.

This is just one way I make faith part of my life every day. This begs the question, "How do we live our faith even through the struggle?" To dig a little deeper, what do you do for your faith on a *daily* basis? I would like everyone to reflect for a short moment about what you already do for your faith on a daily basis.

We each have activities, strengths, interests, things we enjoy. None of us are going to have the same exact ways to live our faith. Some ways we live our faith are chosen or planned — reading the Bible every day; listening to Christian music; or making morning, noon, or night prayer a habit. Other ways are not planned through the "coincidental" experiences and encounters we have on a day-to-day basis. Living our faith on a daily basis means sticking to our planned faith-based activities and acting through God in the unplanned.

If we want to build a relationship with God and show the love we've been given to Him, to others, and to ourselves, then we need to officially make God our No. 1 priority. I heard once in a TED talk, you don't make time for priorities; you set your priorities, and everything else is planned around them.

I was talking to a friend about my faith. While she made many good points, one in particular about Jesus hit me, and it is this: "If He is going to be anything to you, He has to be everything to you." How can He be everything to us?

More often than not, we build our relationship with God through one seemingly ordinary experience at a time. When God's first, the ordinary can become extraordinary.

Tonight, here is my message. If you're struggling with your faith or God's not quite on the most important person on your list, it's OK. Make a commitment with me here tonight to place your relationship with God as your top priority and live the faith, planned and unplanned, on a daily basis. This is a commitment we may need to make every day for it to stick. I know deep down when I examine my heart that I am most happy and secure when my footsteps are on God's path. I think back to times sitting silently in a church or chapel by myself, feeling a sense of calm I have only found in God's presence.

Impact of My Talk

This talk was inspired by not only my leaving the Christian groups at Marywood University but also my struggle with the Catholic view of sexuality. I found it difficult to reconcile my relationship with God and sexual expression. In fact, this is a distinction that would take far longer to understand, but I needed to grapple with church teachings, understand who God is, and manage my own self-criticism to get to this point.

The words I heard during confession from the priest in persona Christi, or in the person of Christ, were especially more important for me to realize came from God. This held an important impact that night at an XLT as well as when I would looked at my phone to see the reminders.

One of my friends who attended this group prompted me to attend a nondenominational church in the area. Sometimes we would attend a Catholic Mass and a nondenominational service on the same day together. My attendance at nondenominational services became significant. I would find God in new ways through the welcoming community, contemporary music, and practical sermons.

A few months later at another XLT event, I ran into the spiritual director for vocations of the diocese. He complimented me on the talk and noted that I should reach out if I ever needed anything. I don't know about you, but there's very few people of status who have told me that if I needed something I should reach out. So I did. Our first meeting was at an Applebee's, the same one I often frequented as my first-date location. My experience of having lunch with a priest in public for the first time was sobering. Priests are people, too. We prayed when the food arrived, which initially made me uneasy. I had struggled with this practice in public but became more comfortable praying at restaurants with friends who shared the same beliefs. He and I discussed my vocation. The meal went on the diocese credit card, which felt like a privilege.

This would be one of many talks this spiritual director and I would have throughout the years about vocations, often about married life. I had no interest in the priesthood, and it was clear that he was steering me away from the single life whenever the topic came up. He was kind and understanding, practical and stern. His words meant something, and often he'd repeat similar phrases and quotes such as, "Good for God, good for us," and St. Julian of Norwich's "All will be well." I appreciated his honesty and willingness to be transparent about his struggles from time to time. He knew about my dating life and that I wasn't an all-star Christian, but then again, I learned that was more common than I realized.

Insight: Transparency

When I used to work at drug and alcohol facilities, I would explain the group rules in detail each time a new member arrived. It was important that my court-mandated clients felt safe enough to participate and understood what was expected of them. I believe this transparency led to greater trust in me and more active participation in the group process.

Furthermore, I don't believe we as therapists are blank slates. I've been encouraged by my circle to share more of what I had to say, and I believe it's part of my gift to share my perspective. I sense that clients appreciate when I'm honest with them. Clients don't want unsolicited advice. However, they do want to know they are understood. Therapists serve a far greater function than a brick wall to be complained at. Someone who can appropriately present a well-informed opinion, in-tune with where the client is, can offer an eye-opening, peaceful experience.

Facial expressions can present as much transparency as words. Sometimes I don't have to say to a client how I actually feel. My clients have seen my looks of disgust, anger, confusion, excitement, and shock many times. Some have even inquired why I made a certain expression. Sometimes I don't mind being quieter in session because I still get my point across. I may express an emotion to a client that is hard for them to acknowledge. I understand that clients may be desensitized to their own stories. They might be well adept at using defense mechanisms, such as distraction, denial, or laughter. Their observation of me sharing my genuine emotional response may help them retune their emotions about what they've shared.

I've also found that being genuinely myself allows for the client's freer emotional expression. For me, a relatively calm counselor, an abrupt curse word or visible frustration gets a client's attention. It may not be the most professional, but it's certainly genuine and might be more meaningful to the client. I also have a tendency to become protective of my clients when it is obvious someone has wronged them. Me raising my voice, squinting my eyebrows, and moving my arms out of anger is analogous to a child telling their mom they were bullied at school and the otherwise kind, caring mother grabbing her purse and saying, "Come on, we're going to find that bully." I've definitely played papa bear or big brother to some clients and have openly admitted this. Knowing some of my clients don't have someone who would stand up for them, I want them to realize that even as their counselor, I can be affected by what happens to them.

No, I don't wither away into a mess or go off the handlebars. We don't actually go and find the "bully." I do my best to empathize without taking on their pain. I've cried with and for clients. I've prayed with and for clients. I've thought about clients when they were celebrating a big moment in their lives, when they were struggling, or when they mysteriously didn't show up for a session. I care about my clients. Yes, counseling is my job, but it is a job you can't do without caring.

No Raises?

Working for ITC was the first time I made enough money to support moving out on my own, which I did within the first few months. The first year I arrived, raises were given, but the second year they weren't. The third year, there was an incentive system based on supervisor ratings. I had the best supervisor there, one who gave me room to work independently. Those who did not receive the higher raises had a supervisor who was much harsher and rigid about paperwork. Generally, it didn't matter, as none of our paychecks were that high as therapists.

The other way to make more money at ITC was to become a supervisor, and I personally had no care to supervise others. I didn't want more work than I already had. To put it in perspective, I had a mini legal notepad which served as my to-do list, and only about a dozen times did my day end with all my tasks completed.

Another reason I didn't want a supervisor position was that I didn't want to be any closer to the CEO than I already was. He spoke freely about current and former employees, even in the hallways. I found this disconcerting and unprofessional. His unpredictable nature also was unsettling. Some days he would laugh and chat about mutual interests, and on others his demeanor was harsh and demanding. His style of leadership was indirect, confusing, and passive-aggressive. He lacked transparency, rarely joining a staff meeting when his and the board of directors' decisions would be announced. It was the supervisors who had to deal with the staff's initial reactions, not him.

Insight: Immense Growth

Clinically, I grew into becoming a counselor. I had some confidence about myself when I arrived thanks to my experience working in a drug and alcohol facility. But connecting to a new population required me to make changes. I went from working with clients with severe levels of substance use to those who had DUIs or drug possession charges. These clients typically had lower levels of substance use. Unlike the experienced clients with heavy drug use who could more readily identify their vices, many of my new clientele initially struggled to admit they drank too much or smoked too often. Many did not admit their offense was *due* to drinking or smoking but rather blamed law enforcement or an event for their situation. Otherwise, they didn't think that drugs and alcohol affected their lives. It was also true that my clients weren't addicted, they didn't need drugs to function, and most of them led productive lives in terms of work/school, family, and relationships. I had to approach counseling differently.

However, my experience at ITC started eerily similar to how my internship at HBC began. In the first group I worked with, I was questioned for not looking like an addict or, put another way, that I didn't belong. This time I had a better sense of how to handle it and felt more confident in myself to not be shaken. Instead, I stayed open. Shortly after, a client discussed the transition of moving, to which another client bluntly asked what color they wanted for the walls or the curtains. The client appeared shocked by this question, as it seemingly had little to do with their initial concern. However, the other client went on to say that we could focus on our worries but really during a change, we have to put our focus on the fun and exciting parts. This was the same client who openly questioned me at the beginning of the group. I knew a special moment had occurred there.

My style evolved to become even more non-defensive and tactical, allowing clients to find what they felt the issues in their lives were with gentle direction from me. I primarily ran wellness groups, which focused on living a healthier and more positive lifestyle. Clinical issues included support systems ingrained with substance use, relationships with faulty communication, difficulty with childcare and work, lack of self-care, and low emotional awareness. I picked various topics, ranging from Maslow's Hierarchy of Needs and the Stages of Change to an analogy of how to balance one's priorities in a way that would produce the kind of silence in which you could hear a pin drop. My clients quickly realized they were not happy with where their priorities were in their lives.

I enjoyed when the culture of a group developed and flowed. When I had a tight-knit group, they welcomed new members. Even once the veteran members left, the new members carried forth the culture of the group. The personalities, dynamics, and stories may have changed, but the atmosphere of the group remained stable and productive.

Insight: Having Favorites & Treating Difficult Clients

I'm going to admit what most of you already know about therapists — especially if you're motivated enough as a client to read a book like this — we have favorites. There are people we connect to like a family member or friend, people whose motivation and insight brings out the best in us, and people whose humor or kindness compel us as they likely do with the other people in their lives. Therapists are biased, too.

We also get turned off by people who push us away. It's not our fault. However, our role as therapists isn't to push away our clients who rub us the wrong way but rather to find ways to connect with them regardless. Acknowledging how certain clients push us away can give us insight into how they may be pushing away others in their lives.

Likewise, certain personality and communication styles might be easier or more difficult for a particular therapist to connect with. I've found that some of the clients who are more difficult for me to work with tend to overtalk, are disrespectful in how they portray their beliefs, are frequently disagreeable, blame others without taking responsibility, display little interest in the therapy process, do not respect my time, and do not listen to what I have to say. Connecting sometimes requires finding a similar hobby, finding a way to agree with their frustration, and identifying positive qualities like their charisma or humor. Understanding what they've been through helps me connect with them, too.

I've had to challenge myself with these clients through setting and maintaining healthy boundaries. My late cancellation/no-show policy has to be upheld, especially with these clients because I know bitterness may start to fester if I push their treatment for too long. I have to be firm and clear about making payments and about the policies they agreed on. I must remain open to send proper referrals when appropriate and treat the person with respect.

Having favorites comes with its own challenges, such as being aware of countertransference, or my feelings/experience of the client in front of me. Becoming too friendly in session or letting clients get away with too many cancellations or a poor structure in therapy can create a detrimental therapy experience in the most unintentional way. Being comfortable with a client does not necessarily mean that self-disclosure becomes most effective. Letting a co-pay or two slide can create a poor dynamic for clinical work. Favorite clients are still clients. It may be necessary to seek consultation for them if you start to see that therapy becomes less effective because of countertransference.

Distractions

ITC seemed to go in cycles. The work would be smooth sailing for about six months, then a terrible management or board decision would happen. These decisions involved the aforementioned lack of raises, a group of employees losing their parking, and no more jeans on casual Fridays. My coworkers and I would jabber about how we hated the place. Simultaneously, we would fear our CEO listening to us through the thin walls of the breakroom. Ultimately, we had to adjust to the new inconveniences we faced with little guidance on how to manage the new guidelines. A couple weeks later after they were implemented, the facility would seemingly and bizarrely go back to normal, or as close to normal as ITC would get.

Burnout from the paperwork alone was real. When I was first hired, we were still using paper filing for notes, which had a tedious process to print, sign, and organize documents ranging from session notes and treatment plans to non-billable notes about rescheduling in three-punch binders. Later, we had an online system. However, the group notes were cumbersome, as we had to add the entire group roster for each session. Writing letters to probation officers was tedious but necessary as it offered a log that recorded whether clients were attending or resembled a cry for help to change strategies. The lengthy discharge paperwork or staff intercomming during sessions became the needles that broke the camels' backs.

What saddens me is realizing how drama and paperwork would occasionally drown out the importance and love I had for my clinical work.

Making the Best of It

I made my own fun at ITC. While I personally hate pranks and don't enjoy scaring people, I have a tendency to walk quietly. From time to time I'd visit a coworker and peek into their office to say hello. To my bewilderment and amusement, they would jump back in surprise, not realizing I was there. This happened enough times that I would walk around the workplace clicking a pen or, as I did at my next job, wearing a key fob with a keychain that jingled so my coworkers could hear me walking down the hallways.

I once wrote the name "Andy" in Sharpie on the bottom of my shoe like how the boy in *Toy Story* does to his toys. Nobody noticed, which was even funnier for me. Sometimes while sitting in a circle during a group, I'd realize my leg was crossed, so the person beside me could have easily seen the name. It was an inside joke I had with myself that few others knew.

Training sessions were a nice way to spend time with coworkers outside of work. On one occasion, I drove to a training while blasting music, my foot bouncing on the gas pedal. A coworker then alerted me to what I was doing. Between that and the less-than-smooth ride, they made it clear that I would not be driving them to another training.

To cope with being in such a hectic, busy place, we just did what came natural to all of us — talk. It wasn't surprising to find me spending a half hour chatting and joking around with my coworkers. Some of these conversations were casual, checking in on how someone was doing or consulting about a case. Other times, they were deeply personal, as I had multiple coworkers who would refer to me as their "work husband." This was a running joke around the office. On one such occasion, I made an impromptu breakroom speech about how if any of my female coworkers' significant others complained about me, they could consider how I gave out snacks, listened when they were upset, and was protective of them without any of the relationship perks their significant others received. The group laughed because they knew I was right.

Token Male

Being the token male in his twenties at ITC was both encouraging and isolating. I felt a sense of pride being protective over my female coworkers, especially when they needed my help. For much of my time there I was single, and this gave me an additional sense of purpose. For me, the title of work husband was a responsibility in the friendships I built.

A frequent issue at my job was a lack of male therapists to perform drug screens. Typically, drug screens had to take place in the presence of a therapist so as to prevent tampering, and you might be surprised at the extremes to which clients would go in order to fake a drug test. There was a fairly detailed procedure on how to have clients prepare for the screen, such as thoroughly rinsing their hands and showing their beltline. We would not actually watch the client pee, but we would stand behind them. This was significantly difficult for clients who were uncomfortable with this process or those who were bladder shy. With the majority of our clientele being male, I was often called from my busy list of tasks to run upstairs, conduct a drug screen, and view the results. This was my least favorite part of my job, and my female coworkers became increasingly aware of my uncharacteristic irritability when they would call.

Despite the pee tests, as a young male therapist, I sometimes felt alone. Finding common interests and ways of communicating with many of my female coworkers was at times uneasy. When they chose to engage in office drama, I would excuse myself or attempt to defuse the conversation. There were times when they would talk about their periods or sexual topics that would make me uncomfortable. I knew they weren't being disrespectful. In a way, I managed to be accepted as one of them.

Yet, I wasn't quite one of them. I preferred at times to talk about video games and sports, topics many of my female coworkers did not relate to. Despite my inclusion in the group, I was left out of invitations to go to lunch or order out. I learned to lean more on my male friends outside of work.

Overall, I appreciated working with mostly women. This experience helped me learn more about what was important for them. I admired them for how they dealt with their struggles, and I feel honored that I built friendships with them along the way.

Insight: Agreeableness & People Pleasing

One of the greatest skills I developed in the field was the ability to find common ground with my clients. In the drug and alcohol field, they often complained about their legal situations. Some found fault with so many aspects of their charges that you would think they were lawyers. Their venting hid their level of responsibility and shame. I found ways to empathize with them about their situations, even if I knew some parts of the story were marred with masks and excuses. I had to first align with a client and build rapport before confronting the hard truths.

In this way, I didn't attempt to challenge my clients right away. Even when I do confront clients, even in my own practice, I try to do it in a way that can be *heard* by my clients. If a challenge is too harsh, it may be pushed away. This includes when I ask a client a question that they ignore, change the topic, or over explain. I find ways to understand what the client is saying and gently circle back to it, sometimes through the use of humor.

I can be more straightforward with my private practice clients as an established LPC than I could as a recent graduate working in drug and alcohol facilities. I lacked the confidence and experience back then to be firm in my words. I had to find my confidence and learn the necessary skills.

As many people pleasers do, I learned people-pleasing behaviors from my family dynamics. I was the "lost child," the one who didn't deal with the conflict directly. As such, my opinions were often left unheard. I even ignored and denied my own feelings. Additionally, people-pleasing served the function of fitting in. This went back to my childhood. While at times people-pleasing can help build friendships and bonds, it ignores hard truths and difficult conversations. Challenging my people-pleasing tendencies helps me better state my own needs and become more confident in my viewpoints. I can still hold empathy and awareness of the other person in a way that is more authentic to me.

Grandpa Passing

One of my more difficult times at ITC was the week my grandfather passed. Growing up, my parents, brother, and I lived on the second floor while my paternal grandparents lived on the first. My peers at school were often jealous of how often I would see my grandparents. My brother and I would play bowling using a kickball we would whirl at toy army men my grandma would set up on the kitchen floor. With my grandpa, we learned to play poker using pennies. His best poker advice to us was to never go for an inside straight.

My grandma passed in spring 2013 when I was a senior in college. I remember her as one of the only people at that time in my life who encouraged me to become more socially involved. Sometimes I would wish she was still alive so I could tell her how I became more sociable and made friends. I felt a special connection with my grandma. My cousin and I theorized it's because I looked like my grandpa.

I made the mistake of going to school the day after she passed, unaware of how strong my emotions were. I silently teared up to myself in the back of a computer room during one of my classes. Then, in my night class, I spent an extended break in the rotunda with a good friend who comforted me, which marked the first time I opened up to someone about my personal problems, at age 21.

My grandmother's death left my grandpa devastated. Family members tried to persuade him to attend parties or help him "move on," but he often isolated himself. I can't imagine how painful it was for him to lose my grandma, especially knowing the kind of loving relationship they had with one another.

He was still mentally sharp for his age but reached a point when he began to physically decline rapidly when he was diagnosed with cancer. While my parents lived upstairs from him, they knew his condition was more than they could handle, and he moved into a nursing home that then transitioned to hospice.

Would you prefer if your mind declined but your body was still intact, or your body declined but you still had your mind? Others in the nursing home with him seemed to have lost their minds first. My grandfather knew that his body was failing and was aware of the sad place he was in.

My last memories of my grandfather were about a month before he passed when my dad, brother, and I visited him. We went to a community room and watched college basketball together. My grandpa seemed to know everything about the sports and teams he followed. He was a fan of the New York Yankees, the New York Giants, and the UConn Women's Basketball Team, especially Brittany Griner. Watching the games with him felt normal, like home. When we left, my grandpa moved his wheelchair toward the door and waved. It was the sort of moment that you want to encapsulate in a snow globe. I had a feeling this would be the last time I would see him.

Not long after, I heard his health was worsening. My parents agreed that my grandfather would not want my brother and I to see him in that condition. I understood, content with the last memory I had of him. I was on lunch break at ITC on April 11, a day before my brother's birthday, when I received the call that my grandfather had passed. I left the lunchroom without telling my coworkers. I went to human resources and told her what happened, that I would run my group and then leave for the night. She gave me a big hug. I ran my group because I felt I needed to. I didn't tell my clients what happened but believed being with them was therapeutic for me. I left that Wednesday night and took off until the following Tuesday, thankful for the time to grieve.

I wept in the shower the next day listening to a cover of "On Eagle's Wings," a song often played at Catholic funerals. I saw my grandfather in the casket at a private viewing and, as the last member of the family to leave the room, saluted him. He was a World War II Navy veteran who had served in the Pacific, targeting where the missiles would fire. He didn't speak much to me about World War II except that he loved traveling in Japan, an opportunity a small-town boy from Dunmore, Pennsylvania, would not have gotten otherwise. My parents at one point chipped in to buy him a framed piece of artwork of his ship, the

USS Pasadena, which now hangs in my bedroom. My grandfather also received a piece of wood from the ship for being a plankowner.

I miss both my grandpa and grandma, and I know they are in a better place. I talk to them about my family and my love life, asking for their intercession to God. They were married for 63 years, so they knew about marriage. I've longed to learn how they were when they were my age, or even in their 50s or 60s before their health declined. I wrote a poem about my grandfather on the two-year anniversary of his death that I called "Gramps."

MISTER ROSS

Gramps (Poem)

My gramps would be 95 today,
    Two years since he has passed,
    Time has quickly come and gone,
    Life comes and goes so fast.

    On the porch he used to sit,
    A sweet smile on his face,
    Waiting for us to come back home,
    To greet us and touch base.

    Knocking on his door to visit,
    He wouldn't hear the knock,
    Walk on in, the door unlocked,
    Loudly you'd have to talk.

    "Hey, little buddy!" he'd say aloud,
    That's what he called us all,
    From my bro to my cousin, even my mom,
    This was his known protocol.

    Once grandma died, it's like he left,
    Only part of him moved on.
    He didn't wish to hear the world,
    For his whole world now was gone.

    Driving to my family's house,
    A flashback right on cue,
    For me he's waiting on the porch
    As he used to do.

BECOMING MISTER ROSS

I think of them both at the grave,
Or when cardinals fly on by,
What love they had, ask God for me
If I can have that before I die.

My Second Baptism

Around this time, I was attending a nondenominational church on and off. At one service, baptisms were being conducted. I watched as members of the church entered the pool on-stage, their stories being shown on the massive screens for all to know their testimonies. I felt emotional and rushed to leave the church first as service ended. While alone in the parking lot, rain fell down on me. In my heart, I felt God saying to me that this was my second baptism, a time of spiritual renewal of my faith with Him. I had felt distanced from Him since leaving college, but this brought me back. He had orchestrated the rain *for me*.

Moments like these seemed to become more frequent. A dragonfly flew by me in the parking lot at work, a rare occurrence that I knew was God speaking to me. When attending one of my diocese's "Leave a Mark" Masses, I was moved to a pew, front and center, unimpeded from others sitting in front of me. God wanted me to know that the Mass was for me in a personal way. My relationship with God became more personal again.

Work With a Spiritual Director

I remained close to my new spiritual director. He deeply cared about me, and he showed it, such as when my one girlfriend left the area to return to her family home three hours away. I was devastated by her move, unsure of what this meant for the relationship and for my own well-being. I was deeply attached to her.

Coincidentally, an appointment was available to see my spiritual director the following day. Upon him asking how I was, I wept for a solid five minutes. It was probably the ugliest cry I've ever had, and he sat there, present with me through it. With her moving away, I felt like I had lost my best friend.

He met this girlfriend on a retreat a few months later as we attempted a long-distance relationship. He was concerned when she broke up with me, knowing how deeply I cared for her and wanted the relationship to work despite our differences in both short-term goals and places in life.

Relocation of priests and deacons occurs frequently in the Catholic church, and it can be difficult to cope with when a spiritual leader you've connected with leaves. Such was the case with my spiritual director. I felt guilty reaching out to him once he left the area and had difficulty finding a new spiritual director. He had recommended a priest, but in meeting with this priest, I felt my need for community was invalidated. He ended up pushing me further away from the Catholic faith through his mistimed sternness and insensitivity to what I was seeking. However, I am honored to have worked with this spiritual director. When I asked permission to use his name in this book, he asked that I did not, wanting the glory be to God, and I respect his wishes.

Chapter Ten
Drama, Politics, and Management
Intentional Treatment Counseling (ITC)

Lack of Leadership

Right from the beginning, the lack of communication and leadership at ITC confused me. Initially, I did not schedule a full caseload each week, as I was told to give myself time to adjust. At my previous job, I had blocks of free time for paperwork. I received a note about my clinical hours that week (hours spent in session) stating that if I did not increase my "numbers," I would be written up. I was already threatened before I knew what I was supposed to do, let alone how.

The company ran on "numbers" — it was the most-used word there. We had to see as many people as we could fit in our schedules each week. We'd be praised when we had high numbers and questioned when they were low, despite the fact that the numbers were primarily reliant on whether our clients showed up, not on our work ethic or clinical competence.

The threatening note mobilized me to take on more intake sessions as well as strategically take on the wellness groups. Like buying both houses on a Monopoly block, I saw it as advantageous to lead both groups. One was passed to me, and another my best friend had, but she was struggling to manage her caseload. I volunteered to take the group from her to ease her workload and hopefully increase my job security. The deal worked for both of us. I loved the wellness group, but I did not like that fear was used to motivate me. I was not lazy or resistant to instruction, but I lacked clear direction and guidance by the management.

I found in my personal journal an entry about another situation regarding management:

"...a supervisor spoke to me at work, stating that multiple sources in and outside the facility shared how I had 'trashed' the place. While this was true I had expressed my disgust to others, I felt uncomfortable with the supervisors knowing and presenting it back to me; but I wasn't angry. I wasn't paranoid or anxious. I was almost at peace they knew, too. This led me to take a step back. I didn't want to complain like that or create a negative environment. This did not mean that I liked my boss or how certain situations were handled. ... I still loved what I did and overall liked my job. I began complaining less and realized that I had made some unresolvable issues even my supervisors couldn't control into beasts in my mind. I was spreading blame and gathering anger inside myself. A change in my perspective made my week great."

I don't know who said what about me, but I was quite opinionated and with good reason. Not once in that conversation was I asked what my grievances were. An opportunity for a productive dialogue was lost. The company sought to silence me rather than to address the problems I had or to even validate that I had them. My acceptance of the situation was what made it better. Management didn't fix the problems I had complained about.

This was a company built on fear. The management was scared to recognize its weaknesses and was unwilling to be vulnerable, while employees were concerned over decreasing job security, losing potential raises if we didn't see enough clients, and dealing with passive-aggressive communication from the management. The company used tactics like this to quiet employees from thinking outside the box or questioning the status quo.

The Board Went First

One incident that best describes the agency's leadership occurred at the annual company dinner held each summer. The board of directors and staff attended, a rare occurrence. No plus-ones or guests were invited, which made the dinner very much a work event, garnished with work talk after a long day at the office. The board, at a separate table, kept to themselves for most of the evening. One of the directors dropped by to compliment us, but their remarks made it clear they did not understand our work.

When the buffet was set, the first table to go up was the board with the CEO at the front. This bothered me. These people didn't have a clue about the clients we served and didn't put in any of the work in the trenches. These were the same people who seemed to change the rules in ways that deterred, not benefited, us. The board members, especially the CEO, were supposed to be the leaders of our company. Simon Sinek wrote a book about business call *Leaders Eat Last* — the board of directors showed otherwise that day. They felt like they were the most important people at that dinner, not us, the people who made the company and helped the clients.

The Closed Door

An incident that significantly broke my trust with the CEO happened one day when I was sitting in the office of my best friend at work. Another coworker walked in and closed the door to talk about a fourth coworker. There was no drama or negativity, simply a story involving them. My boss caught wind of this closed-door discussion and was not happy. He made a snarky remark in passing to my friend and I about having our doors closed. I initially thought he was kidding and teased back, but his tone showed otherwise. My friend went to his office to better understand and rectify the situation, but she came back tearful, telling me that he berated her and expected better of her.

Not long after the incident, both of these coworkers were moved to separate offices upstairs. My best friend relocated to a suite of offices called the "cul de sac," where the CEO told her in a backhanded manner that she would be with better coworkers. Considering her only coworkers in the previous suite were me, a new hire, and a couple of part-timers, it meant that he didn't want her to be with me. I took this as a sign of disrespect. Instead, a coworker who was known to share office details with the CEO was moved across from me, a strategic but petty and completely unnecessary move. Fortunately, we became friends, as I was not going to let the CEO get the best of me. But this showed the sick nature of the CEO's paranoia.

Insensitivity

The proverbial straw that broke the camel's back came at a staff meeting about a client who had died. The insurance company was questioning my paperwork. Pressure was put on the facility, even though I had barely worked with this particular client, hardly enough time to do any meaningful counseling. I didn't know what the cause of death was, and as is often taught in the counseling world, we can't take much credit for our clients' successes or blame ourselves when the worst happens. While a supervisor reassured me of no wrongdoing on my part, the subsequent staff meeting felt like a slap in the face. It slowly turned into an unofficial training, which served only to reinforce that I had done something wrong. I agree with the mindset that we can do better and grow from tragic circumstances, but good leaders would have warned me about this training so I could have taken what was said more from a place of concern than as a personal attack.

Being Fair and My Response

Even though I've been critical of the higher-ups, let me be fair. There were times when they shined, such as during a snowstorm when two of the managers stayed last to make sure everyone, coworkers and clients, had a ride. (That same snowstorm, the CEO was the first out the door.) On another occasion, one of my managers, without hesitation, covered my group on a few minutes' notice when I had to leave because of a headache. Managers held it together when many of my coworkers quit, as there was a high turnover rate. Yes, the supervisors were somewhat to blame for the quitting.

My point here is not to bash the leadership at this job but to bring attention to how flawed leadership can impact not only passionate and skilled employees but also a company as a whole. I want to bring attention to how CEOs and managers at counseling agencies are driving good, motivated therapists away from community care and drug and alcohol facilities and into the safe havens of private practice. I'm sure a similar pattern occurs in other fields, too.

My reaction to this lack of managerial leadership at the time was to become a leader to my coworkers. I would check on them when they were struggling. Deescalating conversations about work drama became commonplace. I had considered going on strike multiple times, including when we lost our parking privileges. However, I believed more strongly that our clients needed us working than picketing in front of the building, potentially giving the facility a bad reputation. Convincing guarded clients of the benefits of drug and alcohol counseling is often a key goal in their therapeutic work. Undermining that process was not worth the cost. Neither was the risk of losing our jobs.

Insight: Counseling & Politics

Political beliefs are bound to be discussed in an average counseling session. Fortunately, I've found it easy to manage these encounters since I'm rarely asked what my views are. As a counselor, I have the unique opportunity to hear the opinions and beliefs of people from all walks of life. I may know more about what the people want than the politicians. While I find little interest in politics, I've found myself able to endorse more complex and multi-faceted views from my exposure to so many others. Most political issues are not simply left or right. In many cases, these issues transcend the political arena, speaking to common and relatable human desires that may not be satisfied with political or legislative action alone.

What I have to remember in counseling is to not allow my clients to stay at the macro or big picture for too long. It's important to discern what is in our control and what is not.

What's important for me in my role as a counselor is to support those going through political issues and empower them at the micro level of their lives. Sometimes with my faith-based clients, I'll tell them how I once heard at a local church sermon that Jesus' ministry covered about a 20-mile radius. The Son of God even worked within a small part of the world (it would become much larger, of course).

I love the quote, "Be the change you wish to see in the world." Help your family, your friends, your community. Do good work at your job, school, or home. Make your part of the world a better place versus looking helplessly at what you can't control. Social media often gives the illusion that we have a further reach than we realize while simultaneously making us feel too small to make any meaningful change. However, we can use social media at times to spread positivity or make others feel heard and belong.

"Team Player"

While at ITC, I felt labeled as a lesser worker because I wouldn't take on extra tasks. I was certainly cognizant of how heavy my workload already was. I balanced my caseload of about thirty clients I saw on a weekly to monthly basis. I ran two wellness groups twice weekly for two hours each session. I spent two hours a week working with clients in the partial hospitalization program. In addition to all that, I completed routine paperwork, such as discharges and case reports for the management, medication management reports, and progress letters for probation with the occasional insurance call. Not to mention the urine tests.

I've seen headlines speaking to the concept of "quiet quitting," or keeping to your own work responsibilities and not taking part in tasks that aren't yours.

There's a line between being indifferent about your work and setting healthy boundaries. Was there some selfishness? Sometimes yes. Maybe I should have taken on an extra client or stayed late to cover a group for a sick coworker. But then again, one more would have turned into many more based on my experience of the work culture. My daily tasks alone were difficult enough. Burnout was a real possibility if I took on too much.

But when I was there, I gave what I could, which was a great deal considering the intensity of the job. I helped my best friend and my many coworkers both personally and clinically. I encouraged interns to shadow me so I could guide them in their early clinical experience. I showed new hires the ropes, including a time that I taught one about the art of taking stuff from an office after someone's employment ends. (You had to wait a given time before raiding the office, but after the Friday that person left, the chair and office supplies were fair game.)

The management didn't know what I did for others behind the scenes. I didn't brag about it. Instead, I held a chip on my shoulder for not being noticed. I didn't seek a promotion, but I at least desired the acknowledgment. This is why the term "team player" was a trigger for me. Often, this phrase is used to manipulate the players into doing the dirty work while the coach and management get their own set of rules. I wanted my coworkers, company, and clients to succeed, but poor management can mislabel an unhappy employee's passion as insubordination or apathy.

I loved my clients, and my coworkers felt like family. Yet, feeling undervalued both in pay and status left me prepared to leave. I received my state counseling license (LPC) in April 2019 and my certification as an advanced alcohol and drug counselor (CAADC) in May 2019. In January 2020, four masters level clinicians, myself included, left.

New Opportunity

Through the help of a friend and a former supervisor, I stumbled upon a group private practice. Courageous Counseling Practice (CCP), in late 2019. I had wanted to pursue private practice *someday*, perhaps once I had worked at a college counseling center for a while, but my interview there went even smoother than the previous two. I was told within a minute that I had the job, that a good word was put in for me, and that's how the process worked. I asked many questions and learned as much as I could.

Initially, I took on a part-time role to build my client base while also working at ITC. While my hours at the new facility were few, it was difficult managing the long days at ITC plus Saturday morning sessions. This was likely my best-kept secret at the time, as only one coworker knew I was there, but the writing was on the wall that I was going to leave ITC.

Time felt against me, though. In order to go full-time at CCP, I had to build a caseload, wait for an office space to open for me, and hope a major insurance company accepted my application. I anxiously awaited the end of this process, ready to make my next move of resigning from ITC, which finally occurred in January 2020.

Insight: Acceptance

Acceptance is one of the most important mindsets you can have. Acceptance of outcomes, whether we label them good or bad. Acceptance of setbacks. Acceptance of unfairness. Acceptance that clients come and go, that some don't pay us or do not show for scheduled appointments. Acceptance that we can do our best and seemingly get nowhere. Sometimes we have a major impact, a little impact, or no impact with what we do. As a counselor, I don't always know if I had an impact on my clients.

Counseling to me is one of the most mysterious fields when it comes to having certainty. When a plumber comes to your house to fix the leaky sink, the plumber knows if they were effective when the sink no longer leaks. An athlete's impact is told by wins, statistics, and accolades. An accountant completes the tax return with numbers in the correct boxes. While we write notes about interventions used and the client's responses, this is from our perspective, not an objective, comprehensive truth of what occurred in the session from both angles. The impact of the session may remain unknown.

I also believe therapy has to be taken as a whole, that the process is greater than the sum of its parts. To point the microscope at one session is missing the point. As many of us therapists know, there are different kinds of sessions. There are intakes and treatment plan sessions, which are mostly regimented, but there also are many unplanned kinds of sessions. Crises in which the client falls apart in front of their therapist. The "I don't have anything to say session," which turns out to be a gold mine of what the client does when they're themselves without an agenda. There are victory sessions in which there aren't any problems and the therapist and client grab the lawn chairs, arms behind heads, reflecting on a job well done. Some sessions revolve around the client's desire to continue therapy. Other sessions focus on the therapeutic relationship as counselor and client communicate about a disagreement or get in-depth about who they are to each other. The culmination of these many kinds of sessions, the therapeutic process, is what makes or breaks therapy.

Saying Goodbye

My farewell speech at ITC came during a staff meeting. I wish it was recorded. I spoke about my time there, used some favorite quotes, and thanked each person there personally. My voice shook in a way it hadn't done so in a counseling room before. I didn't realize how much I would miss having a work family like I had there.

Goodbyes were familiar at the facility. In the two and a half years I spent there, about 25 other therapists and staff members left, many of whom joined the facility after me. This time, though, I was the one leaving. A supervisor caught me in the break room at lunch, the same one who called me out for my complaining a year and a half prior. He applauded me and told me how my speech was much needed for morale.

I had heard before that if someone left the agency to work in another field, it was because they were unfit to work in drug and alcohol. They weren't cut out for it, they would say. But for many of us who left the field, this was not true. For me, issues within the agency, the low pay, and the lack of support during a difficult time led to my departure. We weren't weak. We were undervalued and tired of it.

There was a famous rumor that the CEO was absent on an employee's last day at the agency. In his defense, a person's last day was typically on a Friday when he took off, so this was understandable. To my surprise, he was there on my last day. Whether this was intentional, it was hard to tell. I felt validated by his sending me off and was grateful that we ended our work relationship on a positive note.

He was the same CEO who I once laughed with about an interviewee requesting a $60,000 salary. Who you listen to has a profound influence on where you are going. If I had stayed at that company, $60,000 was laughable. But having left for a group practice and later to start my own business, this number was no longer farfetched but rather reasonably expected. I grossed over $110,000 for 2022, my first full year of private practice.

Naturally on my last day at ITC, I was called to do a urine screen, hopefully the last supervised one of my career. I was informed that this client had been belligerent with a female coworker, which put me on the defensive. I knew I had to stay calm. Upon arriving for the screen, the client glared at me, maybe because he was angry, maybe because I was young, likely because of the celebratory Hawaiian shirt I was donning. He couldn't pee the first time, so I returned to my office.

During a calmer round two a short while later, I was honest with him. This was my last day at ITC, I could say what I wanted about the place, and I encouraged him to give the place a chance. His demeanor completely changed. He actually seemed open to trying out treatment. I don't know who this person was or how treatment would go for them. Often in counseling, we get a chapter or two but never the entire story. In this case, I merely got the first paragraph. Yet, I felt accomplished in planting this seed for him to pursue treatment with an open mind.

I knew I took away some incredible skills from this field. Being able to change someone's attitude about treatment during a urine screen is a testament to what I learned.

Chapter Eleven

Courageous Counseling Practice (CCP)

No Ties

I started full-time at CCP in February 2020. Private practice was a breath of fresh air compared to the drug and alcohol scene. I preferred the greater emphasis on mental health from the start. Meanwhile, the voluntary nature of client participation compared to the drug and alcohol field was refreshing. For the most part, clients actually wanted to meet with me and had goals in mind. Their issues were diverse. I conducted significantly more individual counseling sessions rather than the group counseling I had gained so much experience with.

The workplace environment of CCP was a necessary change of pace. My coworkers were friendly and sociable, similar to my last place. However, I felt a greater sense of leadership from the new CEO and took mental notes on how she created a more positive atmosphere. Communication was direct but I never felt in trouble for a mistake or error.

While work was still work, the offices were more relaxed. Paperwork was structured but not overwhelming. Leather seats and natural lighting made for a more comfortable space. Rather than being told to dress like the expert, I was informed not to wear a tie. Instead, sweatpants were encouraged. This was a stark difference in philosophies. Looking relatable to the client was more important.

Insight: Slow Days

One thing I struggled with at times were slow days. In the counseling agency world, a cancellation means having a free hour to catch up on mounds of paperwork and take an uninterrupted break to go to the bathroom at your hourly rate. In the private practice world, it means you don't get paid. Sure, you have the freedom to do what you want, and this can be nice during a difficult day or week. Some private practitioners have the benefit of charging clients for late cancellations or no-shows, sometimes at half or even the full price of their rate. However, as therapists, we often struggle between our roles as businesspeople and therapists. We want to be empathetic when a client tells us of an emergency, such as an illness or car troubles, but we also have to keep the lights on and hold clients accountable. Additionally, some insurances, such as Medicaid, don't allow for therapists to charge for late cancellations and no-shows. This can become frustrating if the client's reasoning is that they overslept or forgot about the appointment despite multiple automated reminders.

Going to work with a bunch of cancellations is like showing up at your 9-to-5 job and being told that you aren't needed between the times of 10 to 11, 1 to 2, and 3 to 4. During those times, you won't get paid, and there's nothing you can do about it. Most people would be frustrated by such a proposition. This is something self-employed people truly understand. The bills are on us — there's a lot of pressure if you think too hard on it.

Early on in my private practice career, one or two missed sessions would leave me questioning if counseling was a good career choice, if I should build up my caseload of clients, or if I wasted my day. I would worry that scheduling enough clients for the week might push me to overbook other days or inconvenience my own schedule.

I learned I had to chill out when these inevitable events happened. Therapists get paid enough to weather this storm. The bittersweet truth is that there are plenty of people who need help, and that number won't run out. Honestly, I believe that God takes care of me, whether guiding me with helping clients or allowing me to feel financially secure during less busy times, and it reassures me that I've done what He asked me to do for the day. I've decided to take on other tasks, such as improving my business, doing some self-care, writing, and pursuing other projects. Writing this book happened in part with the time and energy afforded to me by cancellations or openings in my workdays.

Acceptance is most important. There have been days I realized I needed the extra hour or two to catch up on my own things. I've made good use of those times. Telehealth has made this process much easier, as I can be at home when cancellations arise with much more to do than if I was stuck at an office. Sometimes you show up for work and there's less to do than you anticipated.

My World Changed

They say things happen in threes. During this time, my girlfriend for much of 2019 broke up with me a day after I moved into the house I bought the previous week. She was the first girl I truly fell for. We were friends who met through a local Christian group. We held similar values, a love of sports, and a shared sense of humor that made interactions easy. I enjoyed spending time with not only her but also her family and friends. Her parents were both pastors who taught me more about faith. In fact, her father sharing a story in a sermon about reading his Bible by a river inspired me to buy a Bible.

My OCD emerged during my transition from ITC to CCP in the form of relationship OCD- (ROCD), a subset of OCD. I was frequently frustrated with the lack of contact in my relationship and would obsessively think about her, her whereabouts, and why she wasn't texting me back. I questioned if it was the right relationship for me, if she was giving enough effort, and if I should say initiate certain conversations with her. I checked for texts frequently, even at times when she was clear she would be unavailable. I became angry with her when I'd immediately reply to her texts and then she would not text me back for hours. It felt as if I kept score to gauge if she valued me.

Our relationship became strained when she moved back home three hours away after college graduation. I felt settled in my life and wanted to move closer to her and build a life together, while she was focused on her internship and securing work. We argued about where we would go next. I became anxious frequently and missed her dearly — she had become my best friend. I wanted so badly to have a plan for when we would be physically closer that I would question her about it often over the six months we dated long distance. She felt this was an issue outside her control, while I felt this was a decision we could agree upon and execute. I wanted to have certainty about where we were going. Finally, she agreed to a plan to move closer to me but backed out a few days before Christmas when she broke up with me.

Meanwhile, the opportunity to go full-time at the group practice was accompanied by my long-awaited resignation from the drug and alcohol position. This meant telling my previous employers, coworkers, and clients the sad news. That heartfelt speech I gave to the staff on my last day came at a time when my world was changing, unbeknownst to me.

Why?

In early 2020, shortly after breaking up with my long-term girlfriend, I felt numb. A friend said I had to let out my emotions. I didn't know how.

On a Tuesday night following family dinner, I drove down the interstate back home. Playing on my playlist was the song "Why Am I the One?" by the band fun. I sang along until I found myself screaming at the top of my lungs. I yelled the word "why" with all the fury and confusion that had accumulated over many "failed" dating opportunities. It was a guttural, visceral, borderline involuntary unleashing of emotions at an intensity I had never experienced. Tears ran down my face as I got to the exit and began to calm down.

This was the kind of catharsis my friend meant. It hurt deeply, and I don't think all the hurt I had felt from my previous relationship was yet unleashed, even with that powerful experience.

The World Changed

A month into having my own office at the group practice, the pandemic began.

Fear. It was a Monday. I remember seeing on the waiting room television that starting at 8PM, restaurants were closing. I went about my business, thinking about my new girlfriend at the time, who was a waitress. I didn't know what any of this meant. Nobody did. It wasn't long before I learned that I was considered "essential personnel." Telehealth went from a concept we had studied to our primary means of conducting therapy. Training for telehealth was offered immediately. In-person sessions continued, and not long after, masks became the norm.

There was debate in the counseling community about wearing masks, with some feeling that clients needed to see our faces to trust us and feel safe. I found myself as an outlier, being one of the few therapists wearing a mask in the building as I prioritized my own health. I hesitated to ask clients to wear masks, as they had differing views on the topic. After I had my first scare with COVID-19, though, asking clients to wear masks for in-person sessions became necessary for my own peace of mind. Other therapists also took additional precautions. Even my clients at the rural office I'd travel to began wearing masks, as the pandemic had hit their small town.

Spring Flowers, Strange Hours

Work was the highlight of my days, rinse and repeat, practically my only way of social interaction besides seeing my roommates. I spent the early pandemic playing video games such as *Animal Crossing: New Horizons* and watching documentaries such as *The Last Dance* and *30 for 30*. I felt nostalgic about a time when people would watch the same show on the same night, feeling as if you were watching the episode with the rest of the nation. Faith-wise, I stopped going to Mass for much of the pandemic and started watching a local nondenominational church's streamed service, which became part of my Sunday morning routine.

The majority of my sessions took place via telehealth, yet there were still in-person sessions that my boss reinforced we had to maintain. Since this contact with clients outside my "bubble" meant I could not see my family, I grew bitter. At times, in-person sessions were refreshing, an excuse to enter into the world that was shut down to many. Other times, in-person sessions were a reminder that I'd rather be working in my sweatpants at home. I also wanted to see my cat and new best friend, Gabby, who became a big part of my life upon rescuing her in June 2020.

Once a week, I drove 40 minutes to a rural office where many of my clients often didn't show or canceled late, making the drive and sometimes the whole day feel like a waste of time. Initially, my CEO assured me that the paychecks would be higher at this office and reiterated my primary building had no office space available on that day of the week. As part of my agreement to work there, I sucked it up and made the drive, hoping for greater opportunities clinically and financially.

During this time, I had frequent, almost daily, headaches, but the worst ones came on Mondays. I wondered why, but I now believe the drive to the other office, the anger that I could not get my own office, and how my experience at the rural location turned out financially all contributed to the headaches. While I felt my work was significant and meaningful to the clients, couples, and families I saw — people I likely wouldn't have met otherwise — I also felt like I was getting shafted financially.

The referrals I received often were for couples. Admittedly, I wasn't as effective as I would have liked to be with couples. In many sessions, one or both of them stormed out of my office. From a clinical standpoint, it was eye-opening. From a financial standpoint, it was annoying, as couples sessions paid less than an individual session at my primary office. The cancellations annoyed me, as some days I wouldn't see my first client until mid-afternoon after driving there in the late morning. My employer questioned my decision to take days off as I

MISTER ROSS

began to schedule more telehealth clients on Mondays and slowly wean myself from seeing clients at the rural office as they either stopped coming or completed treatment.

Gift of Gab (A poem about my cat, Gabby)

Affectionate, a child-like creature,
Love in her soul, sociable, sweetness still,
Indescribable distinctive feature,
Tough tracking down her take for the showbill.
Her eyes like marbles, majestic lime moons,
Her coat clothed in dark cinnamon bun swirls,
Not to be mistaken for a racoon,
Yet nature distinct to one of the girls.
But more complex is she than fair feline,
Awaiting her master's morning entry,
Greetings of purrs and claws as she will pine,
For affection from the local gentry.
To find her place, she becomes a whole cat.
To proceed with her performance, a brat.

Headaches

During my time at both ITC and CCP, I experienced chronic headaches. Most of them I would have rated as low-level, mostly occurring on the left side of my head, ranging from my neck up to my jaw and into my temple and eyebrow. At best, the pain was annoying and, at worst, disruptive to the point where I wouldn't feel able to think.

Here is an adapted Reddit post I wrote on April 11, 2021, about my experience with headaches:

I suffered from nearly daily headaches for about two years and even remember frequent headaches as a kid and teenager, popping Tylenols before a day at school. Here I want to share my story in hopes that it helps you keep searching for a cure or management of your pain because it's beautiful when you find a place with less or no pain. Disclaimers: I'm not a medical doctor and believe that, consistent with those who developed what I'm about to share with you, medical attention should be taken and explored before trying what worked for me. This is not medical advice but my experience with headaches.

My journey is probably like many others looking for answers. I started with medicine. I went to my primary care physician to inform him of pain in my shoulder area that seemed to spread upward to my head. He sent me to an orthopedic doctor. The orthopedic diagnosed me with muscle spasms in my shoulder and bad posture. He sent me to a physical therapist. The physical therapist was confused by how I could have headaches while [I had] aching in my left calf muscle. He had me do a regimen to increase shoulder/neck strength as well as relieve pain through pressure-point therapies. I successfully completed physical therapy with less pain, but not long after, once I stopped doing the exercises and had no access to pressure-point therapy, had headaches once again. I checked with my dentist why I was having pain in my jaw to the suggestion of a mouthguard at night, which did little to nothing. I went to a massage therapist, who stated how many knots I had and recommended I see a chiropractor. I then went to a chiropractor whose only way to contest my pain was massages with pain promptly returning the next day. I tried supplements for pain such as riboflavin and magnesium, to little avail. I tried yoga and exercise, which helped randomly for a time. I spoke to my primary care physician and was given a referral for a neurologist.

Upon less than a minute of explaining my symptoms, the neurologist announced that I had occipital neuralgia. Clear as day he made it sound. A diagnosis I later realize doesn't mean much in my experience. And if there's anything about medicine we should know, it's not to chase symptoms but rather the root of the problem. He recommended a nerve block and there I was, getting four shots in the back of my head. I felt good for a day... then the pain was back. The situation became worse as an unexpected, a nearly $2,000 bill waited for me from the hospital for the shots. Meanwhile, the neurologist suggested separate MRIs for my head and neck, at least $500 a piece out of pocket, to rule out a tumor. He had told me that he was leaving the practice and I would be told about a new neurologist, because if the shot did not help, it may point to other issues. I received snail mail too long after for me to bother following up with another doctor.

At this point I was bitter. But eventually, I needed to forgive. As a Christian, I prayed for the pain to be taken away for quite some time. One day shortly after, I stumbled upon a podcast, *The Cure for Chronic Pain with Nicole J. Sachs, LCSW*. She shared her story about searching for cures for pain in the medical field to stumble upon the work of Dr. John Sarno. The root of pain was not the anatomical or medical problem, posited Sachs, but repressed emotions. While I'm a believer in medical science, I also believe that our emotional and mental states, even if we may not be able to "observe" them like we can a broken bone, can significantly affect our bodies and actually have observable and measurable symptomatology. Why else do we get lumps in our throats, sweaty hands, and knots in our stomach if our emotions didn't affect our bodies? While farfetched, I needed to try [Sachs' approach]. Sachs spoke about JournalSpeak, a way of journaling to work through repressed emotions. She discussed journaling daily and even doing the work in psychotherapy. Her podcast episode about it and four-part YouTube series gave me the information I needed along with Dr. John Sarno's book, *Healing Back Pain*.

Most days, I am pain-free. Granted, I had started doing the work prior to my headaches going away, but now the extra awareness has helped me change my mindset and be more honest with myself on a day-to-day, even moment-to-moment, basis. I had to acknowledge the anger and anxiety I had as a child going to school, feeling overwhelmed from time to time, and being angry at someone so I can let go of the pain. I can recognize when I feel a twinge of pain that I'm feeling overwhelmed or angry, and use the pain to help me while also knowing that the pain does not need to stay, and likely won't once I acknowledge it.

While this treatment may not be for everyone, and some will be against the idea pain can be emotional or psychosomatic, I wanted to share my story that as you continue to search and explore for answers, there is hope. I didn't think it was possible and wondered if I would have headaches for the rest of my life, and now, I feel more able to manage my emotions today and more prepared whenever the headaches may come back.

Money Talks

I wondered how else to make more money besides running myself ragged like some of my fellow therapists who would see twelve clients some days with no lunch. One day in early 2021, a colleague reminded me of the forty percent being taken out of my paycheck. For many group practices, the CEO or owner contracts therapists and splits the pay. For a sixty-forty split, I as the counselor would receive sixty percent of all insurance or client payments, while the other forty percent would go back to the company for rent, use of technology, utilities, and whatever else they needed it for. Part of me felt bitter envisioning money going back into the CEO's pocket, even though I respected my boss and felt she was competent with how she ran the place. I looked at my paycheck and realized the forty percent could have been used to rent three, four, or even five office spaces.

I felt a sense of urgency to leave. I spoke with my financial adviser, my former supervisor Kristy, my counselor, my parents, and my friends. By the next Monday, I sent a letter to my boss letting her know I would be leaving. Soon after, my boss asked me for a timeline. I knew how fast I could work, but I didn't know how fast the insurance companies would credential me. The process for becoming a provider for an insurance company was as straightforward as filling out an application online. However, I was unsure how long it would take for my application, signatures, and online banking to be processed.

Regardless, I had made my decision and was set to leave in June 2021 to start my own counseling practice.

Chapter Twelve
The New Business & OCD Strikes Back

Humble Beginnings Part 2

I set up the foundation of my new business in two weeks, a ridiculous timeline for starting a business. I do not recommend this for anyone and soon faced the consequences of overwhelming myself. Most of my spare time went toward my new endeavor. One late night, I wrote a four-column list on my whiteboard detailing what I needed to do to start my business. My former supervisor informed me of an office space nearby, one where my counselor once saw me prior to the pandemic. The small office with its Smurf-blue walls felt in some ways like a downgrade from the group practice's large office with leathery couches, but I reminded myself that this would be *my* office.

The Panic Attack

Early June 2021, I experienced another major bout with OCD. My significant other at the time and I had been discussing getting engaged. I hadn't let my family or friends know I was looking to get married so soon. A break from the pandemic with the emergence of vaccines brought on more stress than solace. I wanted to be a homebody and had started feeling hesitant about getting back to the "real world." Meanwhile, my girlfriend emphasized how we would be going out and about, a stressful proposition socially and financially. I considered the numbers when it came to an engagement ring, a wedding (knowing her family didn't have the money to afford one), and the cost of supporting ourselves while she worked at a low-wage job. The numbers didn't add up. I also had been struggling with discomfort in the relationship. I questioned if she was fit to marry given her lack of experience living on her own and her lack of initiative in making positive changes in her life.

An illness that brought back bad memories of sinus infections in my pre-teen years led to me losing it. I had a full-blown panic attack. My mind raced with obsessive and intrusive thoughts. My body was overcome with dread and anxiousness. I could barely breathe and shook in the fetal position for so long that it felt traumatic. The woman who I had once wanted to marry looked on helplessly. When she called my parents and handed me the phone mid-panic attack, I knew she couldn't handle a crisis. I instantly lost trust in her. I was alone. I felt my life was over.

My parents fortunately came over to my house late that night and calmed me down. I got an antibiotic the next day, realizing that sinus problems were a trigger, part of the reason for the panic. But the doubts about my relationship crept in, enough to make me cautious. Once my significant other realized I was not as certain about us as I had been, she claimed I had ill intent. Her family turned on me as well. I took off work the next day, as did she, but she did not come to visit. Instead, when we met a few days later, she questioned and berated me, even judging me for not offering to buy her coffee. I felt like I lost my mind, and she wanted reassurance I could not give. She broke up with me a week later, arriving at my doorstep with a box. I laughed in disbelief. I was abandoned. That was the last time we spoke.

Wandering

The next few months were nothing short of a nightmare. My mind would fixate on fears that I didn't know could be fears. Many of these thoughts were about eating, moral issues, contamination, disturbing images of me harming loved ones, and shame. I would argue with these thoughts ceaselessly, seeming to get a short sense of relief before another thought came back, hitting harder than the one before.

Some days I wandered around my neighborhood with a dark cloud surrounding me. I felt tortured by my own mind. In one such instance, I texted my previous spiritual adviser about a fixation on a spiritual idea —, a scrupulosity thought in which I wondered, "Why shouldn't we be spending all our time in church?" I still have the voicemail in which he saw through the obsessiveness and said loudly and clearly, "This is not from God." Meanwhile, I dealt with the loss of my girlfriend, the person who helped me most through the pandemic and was no longer there.

Insight: Grief

When we think of grief, we often think about death. However, grief can be a concept that is far more encompassing. Grief can apply to any significant loss, such as a breakup, broken friendship, or change in identity. Each loss is unique. Losses that I have described so far do include the traditional definition of grief, such as the loss of my grandparents. However, many other losses occur.

Grief involves change. Change by its very nature entails loss. Grief may be part of the way you respond to these changes.

I've experienced many forms of grief, as have most people. When I started college, I was no longer the "easy A student" and had to work for my grades. I changed jobs many times. I went through multiple significant breakups. At this time in my life, grief came during my adjustment to the pandemic-hit world, a change of jobs, and a breakup within a short timeframe. It is important not to discount the difficulty that comes with changes, even positive ones. We may need to be patient with ourselves and our responses to the changes.

Pure "O"

I learned that the OCD I had was called pure "O" OCD. When you think of OCD, repetitive hand washing or checking doors might come to mind. With pure "O" OCD, however, the obsessions are often about thoughts that are not logical and compulsions that are primarily mental or covert. Examples include reassurance-seeking, online searching, or remembering similar situations.

The goal with OCD is to reduce the anxiety caused by an intrusive and typically unwanted thought, such as a mean statement, disgusting desire, or disturbing image. Instead, loops develop in which the compulsions feel necessary for the obsessions to slow down when, in actuality, the obsession becomes worse, like scratching a rash. It might feel less itchy for a moment, but in time, the itch becomes more intense and spreads.

The key is not to scratch the itch, no matter how annoying, disturbing, or confusing it becomes. At its core, OCD is about trying to control the uncontrollable. It involves dealing with shame that even fools people about the real issues in their lives, keeping them from realizing that they are in fact loveable and worthy of connection. I became afraid of the lies in my own mind, some of which felt convincing. I had to learn to see thoughts as happening in my mind rather than "my thoughts."

Transformation Church based in Tulsa, Oklahoma, had a series called "Cuffing Season" in which it discussed the many areas of life that people might be "cuffed" to. Being "cuffed" was described as having an unhealthy relationship with something rather than a healthy relationship that builds faith. If I had to name a Cuffing Season sermon about OCD, it would be called "Cuffed to Compulsions." The sermon would be based around how often those with OCD cling to compulsions, rituals, and worries rather than depending on God, connecting with others, and being courageous.

I've been cuffed to compulsions and fear for so long, witnessing the impacts it can have. I've missed important moments and lost hours upon days overthinking without being present. I've used distraction so much that at times I lost my identity in relationships and hobbies, forgetting my actual desires and purpose. I've let myself down through avoiding fear-provoking situations, sabotaging relationships, scaring my family, and pushing away God.

Of course, most of this was unintentional. I had to survive. My choice became to live a life based on minimizing the bad at the expense of experiencing joy. OCD has brought me to the worst experiences of my life. I feared the worst, and by fearing the worst, I fell into OCD, which ultimately *was* the worst.

Finding Faith

I went from being on top of the world — aspirations of having my own practice, an almost perfect relationship nearing engagement, and many nights of board games, a favorite hobby of ours — to wanting to die. The fragility of my life was apparent, and it was clear that I had not been honest with myself about what it meant to be happy and successful. In truth, I was disconnected and afraid.

I depended on my counselor, Bill, also a Christian. Meanwhile, I had to lean on God more than I had since my near-death experience. I tried to understand more about God's work in my life. I needed to understand how God actually loved me and what real faith was. I spent many days sitting in a quiet church praying and pondering.

Insight: The Island

Counseling, for as social of a job as it is, can be lonely for the therapist. This is true especially for those who have a solo practice. Initially, I felt group practice was a good step for me prior to having my own practice. I wanted to learn from my colleagues and build good working relationships. I yearned for consultation, accountability, and friendship. However, the pandemic led to more telehealth and less in-person sessions. I spent far less time at the office than I anticipated. Paying forty percent of my earnings to be part of the group practice no longer held its intended value. Hence, I was truly working on an island.

The important thing I realized is to not stay on the island. Having colleagues in the field to talk with about counseling can be validating, whether through consultations or casual conversations. Helping others start their own businesses helped me realize we truly weren't on an island but rather on different boats and yachts in the same ocean. We could yell to each other or meet up — no one was too far away for help. Having groups on social media where I could talk with others about issues and find referrals also kept me connected. Belonging to a consistent consultation group can be valuable.

Learning about the field makes me feel like I'm not on an island, too. Reading a counseling book or listening to podcasts can connect me to the author or host and their experiences in the field. Training also holds me accountable in my pursuit of knowledge.

The island is where I learned that I can be a competent counselor on my own. I worked in the field for quite awhile before this step, and I found I could stand on my own two feet. I value solitude and believe it's necessary for growth. I gained the independence to write and enforce policies which reflected my values and concerns in the field. I could structure my schedule in a way that it fit both my clients and me. I don't have to be accountable to a boss. It has been a worthwhile process so far to balance wearing the boss hat and the worker hat, understanding more about how to manage myself.

Invisible

One day during the summer of 2021 stands out as I dealt with OCD and grief. I can't say I remember what triggered what I was feeling, but an overwhelming sense of dread and depression crept over me. My roommates and I hosted a movie night to watch *Space Jam: A New Legacy*. As a LeBron James fan, I looked forward to seeing one of the greatest athletes of our generation act in a reimagined classic. But my mind plagued me throughout the film. Obsessions entered my mind, and I remained distracted as I dueled with them. Afterward, our two friends went home, and my roommates went to bed. There was just me and Gabby.

I noticed my cat looking at the blank wall by the stairs, seemingly convinced there was someone or something there. I believe she was noticing angels. I went to bed in an awful state with Gabby sleeping beside me for most of the night. I woke late and decided to go to a local park I knew was close to a hospital.

I questioned if I should check myself in. As a therapist, I was aware of the limitations a hospital would have in helping me. It couldn't take away the intrusive thoughts, compulsions, or grief, but it could give me medication and get me through the next 72 hours. Meanwhile, I experienced suicidal thoughts encouraging me to crash my car. I thought about veering over the line into an oncoming car. I considered this option seriously enough to concern me.

The best description of how I felt wandering through the park that day was that of an invisible shadow, lurking unnoticed with a dark essence. Walking along a path, a woman said hello to me. I didn't greet her back, but tears formed in my eyes. Someone noticed me.

I strayed from the path and up to a statue of Abraham Lincoln where my ex and I had played a board game together in the spring. I became emotional and, in a later conversation with my counselor, wondered aloud why I would have gone to this statue. He told me simply that I needed to. He was right.

I drove to my parents, who lived fairly close by, and expressed to them what was bothering me. I cried for four hours that afternoon. I let them into my inner suffering more than I ever had before, and they understood enough for me to feel validated and held. The catharsis was necessary. With that, I went home. The same day, my roommates' father went to the hospital. Not long after, we got into a conflict with a friend. It was one of the worst days of my life.

Yet, it was clear that God had my back. He took care of me through Gabby and my parents, who were truly my best friends during this time. He had His angels watching over me — I am sure of it. I did take an anxiety medication temporarily, which significantly helped me on some rough nights. The dread and feeling that I was invisible subsided, as did the suicidal thoughts. Regardless of feeling alone and unnoticed, I was found. There were ninety-nine sheep and on that day, I was the one who was rescued.

"Real Faith" & Hope

I can't believe I'm the same person. During the season that preceded the panic attack, I lived in a fantasy world I conjured up. I hid in the shadows of the lifeless, coronavirus-fearing world, working on autopilot as a therapist. It concerns me to think of how little I was present with my clients. I spent nights playing games with a girl and pretending the world was perfect when it wasn't. Her personality felt like a mirror, showing me what I wanted to see, not reflecting who she truly was. I wasn't listening to God as much as I thought I was, nor was I trusting Him at the level I needed to for the next stage in my life. I had few genuine connections because of my lack of vulnerability.

As traumatic as the panic attack and my ex leaving me were, I'm thankful these events happened. I needed to be shaken back to reality. God used a difficult time to bring me back to Him. He held me in His arms the whole time; I don't doubt that. I questioned His goodness but didn't question His presence. I can say through great discernment that God is certainly good. In time, I gained hope, which is one of the most beautiful gifts of faith. Even in the midst of our darkest times there is hope, not only of something great but also that someone greater is right there with us. His protection and presence truly motivate and reassure me.

My own mental health struggles gave me a renewed sense of mission and purpose as a counselor. The dread and sorrow my clients talked about I understood more now than before. I wanted to help others get through the difficult times the way my family and counselor helped me get through mine. Likewise, I wanted to share the love God gave me to those He's put on my path.

Insight: Purpose

I'm finding that even with a job that drips with meaning and purpose, it can be easy to wander away from my calling. Burnout, office drama, stress, selfishness, unethical behavior, power, and status have pulled me from my career. I've fallen victim to focusing too much on financial gain, the need for validation, and the desire to appear like an expert. My fears and insecurities have kept me from being vulnerable at times, which can in turn prevent my clients from becoming more vulnerable with me, too.

Personally, in my first six years on the job, I can admit I struggled with sticking to my purpose. Initially, I came into counseling as a bright-eyed, eager student ready to help others grow. Immediately, I was knocked off my horse when I realized many of my clients did not want help. Some were against the system, others were personally unaware, and an unfortunate few had already chosen to live a lifestyle that was not consistent with the healthy practices counseling taught. My efforts were repeatedly thwarted and pushed aside.

Once I began to see what independence and financial freedom in counseling looked like, I had a new direction. I was excited. But this clouded my clinical work. I forgot what it was like to feel needed as I added more boundaries with clients. I grew more bitter about cancellations and how clients disrespected my time. I was angry at how the pandemic was affecting my life. I hated how I had to drive forty minutes to a rural area for what I was told was a better financial opportunity to earn less.

My purpose shifted quite heavily in starting my own practice. As I wanted to pursue even more financial security and independence, I found how much I needed my own counselor. This renewed my clinical purpose of counseling, allowing others to depend on me with more vulnerability. Over time, I've improved at managing frustrations about cancellations and no-shows. I've accepted my clients' varying approaches to counseling, pushing aside my own agendas and rigidity when necessary. Speaking my mind and trusting my judgment have played an important role.

My purpose in counseling is ultimately about serving my clients. It's OK to spend a few extra minutes answering a client when they send a distraught text or listening to a referral on our first phone call. God might want me to do more than I had set out to do. Not everything I do with my work will necessarily make me money or have the outcome I want. But I can rest assured that my work thus far has mattered.

COVID-19 & OCD

COVID-19 gave me a new perspective on how I viewed OCD. Our collective mindset during this fearful time represented a societal level of OCD and in turn contributed to my own. There were many rules, some of which felt arbitrary and driven more by fear or political decisions than science. Frequent mental gymnastics surrounded the topics of exposure, symptomatology, and safe social practices. Overall, people wanted to know they wouldn't harm their loved ones or themselves.

Meanwhile, the news of a vaccine was an emotional rollercoaster as many of us hoped for the end of the pandemic. What we got was disappointment that not only was the vaccine not stopping the pandemic but also that there was stark disagreement on its usefulness, appropriateness, and fast release to the public. Anger already existed toward a faceless virus, but now bitterness arose among family, friends, and communities. And then one day, the pandemic was over?

Among the memories that stood out most about the pandemic were dropping off Easter dinner with a wave to my then-girlfriend, then having Easter dinner with my roommates, isolated from my family. I celebrated my birthday that summer on the opposite side of my parents' porch as the rest of my family. I remember getting yelled at by a Walmart employee when I touched a cart that was not cleaned. From the counseling side, I wore masks in counseling sessions, which was both stuffy and impersonal. The eeriest memory was getting tested for COVID-19 in an abandoned movie theater, waiting for results among the allegedly "infected." I felt like we were bunkering down from a zombie apocalypse, hoping we weren't the ones who had turned.

Having said all that, there are some key similarities in how we were encouraged to think about the pandemic and how those of us with OCD sometimes think. For example, thinking about the "what-ifs," or hypotheticals involved with a situation, is common in OCD. With the pandemic, these "what-ifs" usually pertained to exposure to the virus and when this may have occurred.

If a person touched an object they deemed "contaminated," then they might fear that contaminant spreading to the next object they touched or becoming sick. Meanwhile, obsessions played off the feeling of dirtiness, triggering anxiety. Rather than manage the anxiety and allow thoughts to move along, though, OCD says to follow a certain set of guidelines or rationalize a certain thought in order to make the anxiety go away. Someone might feel compelled to wash their hands, use a disinfectant wipe on the objects they touched, or rethink whether there was a contaminant on an object. The anxiety then returns when this is not done "perfectly" or the next time a similar situation occurs.

OCD thinks it's doing us a favor in keeping us safe and preventing life disruptions. The obsession itself becomes the feared consequence. An obsession is, at its root, a thought, and thoughts in and of themselves are not necessarily true. I've struggled at times working my way out of the OCD thinking that seems to have emerged with the pandemic. I'm an intelligent person with a good memory. If I wanted to, I could backtrack certain behaviors and events in a mental review. That can be helpful when remembering conversations with friends or clients, but when worrying about whether I got cat litter on my hand and touched the garbage can and then touched my other hand which touched the door, well, it's not very helpful. In fact, it's annoying and frustrating.

During the pandemic, I would mentally recall how often I was with a person if I heard they might have COVID-19 or were exposed to the virus. I would check guidelines frequently to ensure I would not harm another person. I hid from my roommates in my room for days on multiple occasions. I even canceled plans with good friends from out of state.

What I failed to realize at the time was that there were healthy ways to manage the virus. If I tested positive for COVID-19, I would stay home for a few days and get better — that would be within my control. If a friend-of-a-friend whom I saw contracted it, though, I wouldn't be able to control that. Instead of thinking rationally about whether I might have the virus, it would have been better for me to manage my anxiety about uncertainty and lack of control.

Contamination OCD plays off shame. For example, I would think that I should have washed my hands extra if I thought I had a contaminant on my hand, for fear that others may touch that contaminant too. They would think

I was inconsiderate if they found out, and I would think of myself as an inconsiderate person. Or if I happened to not wash my hands properly after going to the bathroom, then ate something, that I would somehow become a bad or gross person. In reality, I know some people rarely wash their hands, and while I might find that a little gross, I don't shame people who do that.

I wash my hands fairly frequently, and sometimes it's easier to give into needlessly washing them a little longer than to accept the uncertainty that there is a molecule of a contaminant on my hand. I must realize that I'm not a bad or dirty person either way. It's a struggle for me to find the balance between clean and obsessive. As with the pandemic, there came a point where we all had to find that line of when we would take precautions and when we would let our worries go.

Acceptance & Serenity

This is where God is found in acceptance — the realization that God is the one in control of what's going on, as it states in *Alcoholics Anonymous*, also known as the *Big Book*. I pray a shortened version of the Serenity Prayer originating from the theologian Reinhold Niebuhr, although the full version has even more wisdom:

God, grant me the serenity to accept the things I cannot change, courage to change the things that I can, and the wisdom to know the difference. Living one day at a time; Enjoying one moment at a time; Accepting hardship as the pathway to peace. Taking as He did, this sinful world as it is, not as I would have it. Trusting that He will make all things right if I surrender to His will; That I may be reasonably happy in this life, and supremely happy with Him forever in the next. Amen.

This is OCD's biggest challenge: accepting what is and finding our role in the situation, if any. A thought is a thought, and I don't have to act on it, reflect on it, or consider why I experienced it. If I were to get sick and have an inclination it's COVID-19, maybe I should get tested. If I have an illness that I legitimately think needs medical attention, I should set up an appointment.

MISTER ROSS

But giving myself a COVID-19 test on a "what-if" or messaging my doctor on the off chance it's something serious when, if I'm honest with myself, I know it feels like a cold, that's choosing the obsessive. To follow compulsions offers the reward of short-term relief but punishes with delayed freedom.

Chapter Thirteen
Mister Ross Counseling LLC

My Own Practice

As my end date with CCP approached, I was determined to get my new business off the ground. I called one insurance company almost daily, knowing many of my clients who chose to follow me were depending on this process to continue therapy. I received a contract from the company that I could see its members but without pay until certain paperwork had been completed. This was nerve-wracking, as I knew I would not be paid for quite some time at best, or at worst, I would spend half my work hours doing charity. This was noble but no way to make a living. That I felt nervous was an understatement. I felt the weight of the world on my shoulders to make all this happen — for my clients, for my business, and for me. My livelihood depended on it.

Fortunately, other insurance companies came through. New clients began to reach out. The critical paperwork was completed, and I received a fat check for a month and a half of claims. Business was booming, and with fewer hours of work, I was making more than I ever had. I had more free time. I was still on an island, but I gained the independence I wanted. Work was meaningful again, and I felt awakened.

During this time, I saw my own counselor, Bill, sometimes twice a week to get through. I needed that, and fortunately I was stable enough to be present with my clients. My business wasn't all about finances and independence as it had started. Rather, it was built on allowing clients to work with and depend on me in a similar way to my dependence on my counselor. While I knew the importance of a counselor, this approach felt more significant. I needed my counselor more than ever, and I realized there were clients who needed me like that, too.

Insight: Faith

My story about mental health can't be separated from my faith journey and testimony. I began thriving far beyond my wildest expectations by the grace of God. Trusting Him has been critical for my mind, body, and soul.

Clinically speaking, two main purposes of therapy are to decrease symptomology and increase well-being. There are many ways to achieve both. In my belief, both are possible but admittedly more difficult to achieve without God and faith. As a counselor, I take on many people who are not believers, and I do not push my faith on them. My typical approach with spirituality is to ask at intake what the person's experience with religion and spirituality is and to offer an invitation to explore that deeper. Most times, we do not return to this topic unless the client brings it up.

This is not to say that faith leads to a life free of suffering. Many Christians and people of various beliefs understand this. Jesus Himself stated in John 16:33 (NLT), "I have told you all this so that you may have peace in me. Here on earth you will have many trials and sorrows. But take heart, because I have overcome the world." Who better to have on your side than God?

Mysteriously, some clients have turned to God during my work with them and told me about it. I've witnessed clients who turned to God and had things suddenly work out easier. I know it's no coincidence. This adds another layer onto the work we already do, knowing that faith is part of their process and their relationship with God is open to being addressed.

Sadly, for so many people, the stories are very similar — a person grows up with a particular religion but turns away. Their reasons include negative experiences with the faith, misconceptions perpetuated by preachers and congregations, and the question of suffering. Our suffering. How can there be suffering if an all-knowing, all-loving God exists? I tackled this question in my "Philosophy of Religion" course in college. I won't tackle this issue in detail here; however, it was eye-opening for me to realize through that class, personal experiences, and many sermons, that suffering serves a purpose. We struggle when we are disconnected from God, from others, and from ourselves. Suffering serves to connect us.

Time and again I've been amazed as to how my suffering served a purpose and was relieved by the presence of others. I'm a counselor because I suffered from mental health and because I knew others suffered, too.

The pain caused by the pandemic, my panic attack, and the breakup led to deeper connections. Connections with my family and loved ones have played major roles in me getting back on track. Finding community with others who shared similar values and interests have kept me feeling as if I belonged. And of course, my parents, my cat Gabby, and my counselor Bill helped me feel the most understood.

I'm thankful to God for putting such amazing people along my path. Finding God especially has been like reconnecting with a best friend and realizing it was peaceful spending time with Him. Furthermore, there is a certain sense of peace and direction that can only be attained through faith. To reiterate a quote I shared earlier from a priest, "We have as much faith as we need." I've understood this as not needing to pursue perfection with religion or try to be the most faithful person to pray. Instead, I can turn to God when I need Him and do my best along the way.

Meanwhile, my suffering and journey with God prompted me to place more importance on my relationship with myself. Reconnecting with myself required me to see myself as an important person in my life. This means living in a way that shows love and appreciation for who I am. I was led to put myself in healthier situations and choose to associate more with people who make me better. I make better choices when I am connected with God, the people He has put in my life, and myself. Finding the balance of connecting with God, others, and myself has been challenging, but I'm reassured it's far more rewarding than only having one or two of the three.

Insight: Living with OCD

The worst part about living with OCD is its unpredictability. When I watch a show, I don't know if they'll say something against my beliefs or show something gross that triggers my OCD. When a friend uses God's name in vain, obsessive thoughts occur about whether I should stand up for God and if I'm a bad person if I let it slide. As a counselor, I don't know what my client may share. When a significant other might be flirting with me or initiating sexual acts, I may obsess over the religiosity of the situation rather than share how I authentically feel about connecting with them. During day-to-day tasks, I might obsess about hand washing if I pick up something off the ground or touch dirty laundry. I usually don't set out to think about these things, but they happen in the background. Sometimes I ignore them; sometimes I give them more attention than I ought to.

When someone asks about your day, these are not the kinds of things you tell them. I wonder if my headaches some days are from overthinking. I feel exhausted or unhappy when these obsessions become worse on more stressful days. I've dealt with enough background noise throughout my day that I couldn't tell you what song was metaphorically playing. Some days are easier than others. OCD is best faced through not engaging with the obsession and coping with the anxiety rather than using compulsions to silence the thoughts. This is how you do not allow the thoughts to get the best of you. This is easier said than done when you fear the worst happening if you don't bring some kind of control over the obsession.

It's a battle I often fight alone, although I know I have God, and there are a few people in my circle who know and understand. But most people don't even know what OCD is, let alone my struggle with it. They think it's a love of cleaning, a quirky personality trait, or a funny acronym. In reality, it's more like feeling that you're crazy even when having the same thoughts as everyone else, except others can let go of these thoughts much more easily while someone with OCD has trouble letting them go. OCD is feeling certain that no one would understand and shaming yourself for it.

Unless I explain it to you, I can't expect you to understand, hence this book. I wanted someone to understand. I can imagine my readers with OCD or other mental health issues would like someone to understand their struggles, too. I worried that I was crazy, as you may have. It's validating to realize that your stress and unhealthy habits are the result of a disorder or an issue in your brain and not some inherent problem with you.

The Great Roommate Dissolution

In September 2017, I moved into my first apartment with two of my closest friends from college, lovingly known as "the twins." Our friendship started in undergrad. I met them at a bowling fundraiser but didn't reconnect with them until a year later at Men's Group, the religious group I co-led. Our first week back for the fall 2014 semester, I went to a trivia night with them and a group of friends, then back to their dorm room, where we fought with lightsabers in the dark. I finally felt like I was living the college experience. If you chuckled at that, listen — you can keep your college experience. I like mine.

Following graduation in 2015, when I earned my master's degree in psychology and the twins graduated with their bachelor's degrees, they moved into a local duplex with two friends. I finally had friends from college who stayed local and hung out with them frequently. When the time came for their roommates to move out in 2017, I had just secured my first full-time position and took up their offer to live with them. We resided at that address for nearly two and a half years, during which time they taught me the ropes of living on my own. They pushed me toward community over independence and resting over worrying. These were hard lessons for me to learn.

In December 2019, we moved into a house I bought about two minutes away from our duplex. A number of reasons led me to buying the house. My parents had recently renovated their downstairs apartment, previously my grandparents' residence, for my brother to live in. A potential backup plan was gone if we lost the duplex. Growing frustrations mounted with duplex living, as the next-door neighbors played music on holidays and special occasions that was so loud it shook the walls. Meanwhile, my girlfriend at the time agreed to move back to the Scranton area as part of a plan we built together, which made it feel necessary for me to settle there. Additionally, I gained a growing interest in finances. Buying a house made the most sense across the board.

Fortunately, buying a house was the best move I could have made because of the state of the housing market and low interest rates at the time. Walking into the house during a tour, I felt within 20 minutes that this was my home. I had a dream around that time that God called me on the phone, and the number that came up was the same as the address.

My roommates and I moved in on a frigid Saturday in December with the help of my family and a group of close friends. A day after moving in, my girlfriend broke up with me, our plan gone. Oddly enough, I felt a deep sense of peace as the Facetime call between us ended. God had brought me to this place, and I was OK.

We lived there together until January 2022, enduring much of the pandemic by each other's sides. My relationship with the twins changed as our values and interests evolved. Conversations became more difficult as a two-on-one dynamic developed, their stance against mine. Because of my efforts to make it "our house," I did not feel like this was even "my house," despite my roommates' frequent attempts to empower me to make house-related decisions and encourage me to use the common areas as I pleased. I had given them two rooms to my one and spent little time outside my bedroom, which doubled as my home office during the pandemic.

Romantic relationships and COVID-19 played a significant role in the difficulties with our friendship. As each of my roommates began to bring dates or girlfriends to the already crowded house, I began to feel pushed out and frustrated despite their communication about having guests over. I came to realize that this was my house and that I didn't want to cater to my roommates the way I did previously. Meanwhile, issues with COVID-19 began to strain the relationship. I was more fearful about the virus than my roommates were.

During Thanksgiving 2021, both of them were exposed to COVID-19 and called to notify me on their way home. I was petrified and angry at the idea of spending the next however many weeks isolated in my room because we would have to take plenty of precautions, through no fault of my own. Fortunately, my dad was over at the house that day working on a project. He walked me through some ideas, one of which was to stay with my parents for a short time. This helped me realize that this was my house and I did not want to run from my problems. I put my foot down that I did not want my roommates to come back to the house until they were cleared, a difficult but necessary decision. They made arrangements to stay at an aunt's vacation house and both ended up catching COVID-19.

I spent the next couple weeks realizing how much I loved being on my own, feeling a sense of freedom and acknowledging that the roommate situation was no longer working as it once did. I bought and put together a new TV stand and began making plans about how I would confront my roommates about my decision to have them move out. This was a major step in my independence and focusing more on what I wanted rather than on pleasing other people or avoiding conflict. My roommates had become my brothers, and it was a better choice for myself as well as for our friendship that we moved on.

Insight: #BigMoney

One of the fears when I decided to pursue the field of counseling was that I wouldn't make much money. Previously, my parents and I were excited by the starting salary of a school psychologist. But counseling money to an outsider didn't feel sufficient. I assured my parents I would make it work. I realized there is most certainly money to be made in therapy — six-figure kind of money — which I'm proud to say I made for the first time in 2022 with my own practice.

Think about it — if you asked your family and friends how much they'd want to be paid to listen to other people talk about their problems, I imagine their suggestions would be even higher than what me and my fellow therapists make.

Comedy

With the pandemic winding down yet its impact still felt, I was in search of community. I needed some laughter. I talked with my counselor about how I didn't have the opportunity to perform in my college's improv group, to which he stated that I should pursue comedy. I reached out to a local improv performer who led me to the United Citizens Brigade, a comedy school with locations in New York City and Los Angeles. Conveniently, it offered online courses.

I took two improv classes: one on character monologues and another on sketch writing. I met many aspiring actors, comedians, and performers through these online courses. My background and intentions may have been different from the majority of my peers, but in time, I felt like an equal. On more than a few occasions, I'd make my classmates laugh, and I'd learn the nuts and bolts of comedy that had previously confused me. I gained enough confidence to get out of my shell and not worry so much about getting things right, a significant blow to the perfectionism I once held dear.

I attended classes even when I wanted to quit or pretend I wasn't there. The important part was that I kept showing up despite feeling overwhelmed, dismayed, and disappointed in myself. Rather, I found opportunities to enjoy myself. I began to challenge the creative barriers I once had as well as find the lines of what I found was not appropriate to joke about.

My favorite moments included reading one another's sketches in sketch class, performing with my Improv 101 group, and performing a character monologue of the "Crocodile Hunter," Steve Irwin, in a sketch where he was informing the public about the dangers of COVID-19 as if the virus were a wild animal. If you do a deep dive, this can be found on UCB's YouTube page along with my not-so-funny Improv 201 skit.

The pinnacle of my short comedy career came at a local bar in Scranton in June 2022, when I performed my first stand-up set at an open-mic event. I received chuckles from a friend who recorded the show for me and from a difficult-to-please audience. Bits included me sharing how I got sunburnt at the dentist, pointing out the contradictory nature of the city's potholes, and suggesting whose sculpture should replace the one Christopher Columbus downtown. My heart was racing, but I got through and rode off into the proverbial sunset. I retired from comedy, and that was the last time I was funny. (I'm kidding, obviously.)

Insight: Use of Humor in Counseling

One underrated part about counseling is the use of humor. Well-timed humor in a session is essential. Clients often bring their own humor. For some, it's a necessary form of coping. I've even encouraged some clients to try stand-up comedy with some of the lines they use. With others, light teasing about a vulnerability could open up an important conversation. Laughing naturally lets down our defenses and helps us connect with others. If you can laugh together, maybe you can work together, too.

Consider the context you're working in. Therapy for many has been introduced as stressful or taboo. People may come into counseling with negative therapeutic experiences, sometimes involving a therapist who was disconnected from them. Humor can offer much-needed catharsis, genuine connection, and a new perception of a therapist as a person, not simply an expert or medical professional.

I've noticed that the sessions in which my clients laugh the most also tend to be the ones in which they cry or express feelings the most. Observing what is hidden behind the laughter may be my first step in unleashing what lies deeper. However, this approach must be genuine. If I laugh along with a client, it must come from authentically finding what they're saying to be funny or a strong desire to match their mood. Finding when to laugh at a client's jokes about themselves or their situation also proves difficult. There are times when laughing together in session is connective, while other times it is enabling and distracts from the real work. Sometimes what the client is laughing at is literally terrible and not funny at all. I may offer a deadpan reaction or an empathetic expression to show how I actually feel about what they said. I know we can become desensitized to our own suffering, and a different response from me may break that.

I pace the humor with the deeper stuff. I've seen clients use humor to distract from the subject at hand. Knowing when and how to bring them back from humor to vulnerable material takes proper discernment and awareness of the therapeutic relationship. This isn't Session 1 dynamics. It's built over time.

Difficulties and struggles tend to be the best sources of humor for many comedians. In therapy, I've heard stories that couldn't be made up. Humor isn't necessarily found in the fact that a situation is funny but rather that it does not fit the logical, reasonable flow of events — a sad, peculiar irony. Laughing is the main way many clients learn to cope, especially when circumstances are so difficult that they can hardly believe this is their lives or that they made it through.

Insight: OCD and the Holidays

My OCD typically ramped up on holidays and special occasions. My Christmas Eves as a teenager were ravaged by obsessions about gagging or disrupting family dinner and it being remembered. Birthdays in my adolescence were full of fear about the restaurant we might go to or if I would like the birthday cake. For one of my grandfather's birthdays, I obsessed for two weeks about the restaurant and ended up not going, stating that I didn't feel well. During my own birthday in 2021 while recovering from my breakdown, I feared if I was worth celebrating.

A frequent New Year's Eve worry has been about what my first thoughts of the new year will be and what impact they might have. If I were to think of a word or person I didn't like, I might worry that I'd feel as if I didn't want to live that year. At one particular wedding before I knew I had OCD, I obsessed about whether my hand was clean after I went to the bathroom and, of course, its impact on the wedding.

OCD not only tells you to have as much control as possible but also to do so when specialness is involved. My OCD is also driven by shame, whether brought on by others or myself. The overarching fear is that if I were to mess up in some area on a holiday, I would remember and associate it with that holiday whenever I thought of that day. At its worst, the next holiday would be negatively impacted. Fortunately, I've learned that these fears don't have a bearing in reality and to resist engaging with the obsessions. It's better to push the envelope on some of the OCD rhetoric, although admittedly this is as difficult as it comes.

Typically, people have the mindset of wanting to get a special day such as a holiday, birthday, or wedding "just right." Christmas in America is built on weeks, sometimes months, of build-up with sales, decorations, and planning. Birthdays may require making it the best day for that person, which may mean giving special treatment, buying a great gift, or avoiding arguments. Weddings are often prepared for extensively at a high cost to make it one of the best days of the couple's lives.

Even hosting a party, which can be considered its own special event, is difficult for me sometimes because I want things to be cleaned a certain way. I fear contaminating a surface or object that others may touch, seeing myself as inconsiderate for not having cleaned it. At one Friendsgiving, I obsessed over the fear that I got cat litter and potentially cat poop on my hand, that it then went on the soap dispenser when I washed my hands, and then onto the towel a friend used later. My thoughts triggered the worry that when he was passing around a spoon at the table, people could get sick, in particular a pregnant friend and her baby. This is how far my thoughts can go. In the moment, this felt like a legitimate fear. Logically, though, I knew nothing bad was going to happen. I wasn't convinced my friends would die, and I didn't dive across the table to wash the spoon or demand my friend wash his hands with a new towel. Yet, enough anxiety built in me that I felt the need to argue it away, even if it meant replaying scenes in my mind over and over. I rationalized the situation at the expense of being present with my friends.

But that's what OCD does — it takes us away from the present moment to "protect" us. But truly it's not protecting anyone. I get caught up in arguments in my head, sometimes to the point that it makes me sad how much I haven't truly been in the present. And there really wasn't anything to fear.

Insight: Faith & OCD

I found that with my OCD, each time I reached out to God, He delivered. During the few months immediately following the panic attack and breakup, God gave me signs, connections, and peace. For a couple days, I ruminated about the morality of big businesses if they sold cigarettes. My counselor Bill was there, and he helped me to see that God could be working even through cigarette sales, as he shared how an in-patient facility would sell them for a greater cause. The world was not as black and white as my OCD brain portrayed it.

He introduced me to the AA section of the *Big Book on Acceptance*, which has to be one of the most powerful excerpts of a book I've read. I needed to accept the world as it was and that God had things taken care of. Sure, I had a responsibility in this world, but not to the high degree my OCD would have me believe I did.

My obsessions have gone in many directions. One night during the summer of 2021, I went to a baseball game with a friend. Despite me obsessing about water being too expensive to buy there, he bought some for me. Again, I was taken care of. Walking around the stadium was the respite I needed.

On another night when I felt my obsessions taking over, I walked through the downtown for the monthly First Friday art and music festival. I ran into more people I knew than I thought I would, feeling a sense of connection that shined a light in the midst of the deep shame I felt about my OCD. My OCD could make me feel as if I was a strange mess of a person, yet the reality was that I belonged to a greater community. The obsessions began to fade away.

Multiple occasions at church have brought me peace. Once, I was feeling anxious following a trip to a flea market, thinking that I would be cursed for ten years for not standing up for God when I heard His name used in vain. That kept feeling more convincing than I was comfortable with. Receiving the Eucharist at church that afternoon, though, felt incredibly calming and allowed me to walk home freed up. Sitting in quiet churches have led to important realizations, too.

God has found a way to be there for me consistently, even through the worst of my OCD.

Brainspotting

Brainspotting acted as a reawakening for me as a counselor. Kristy, my previous supervisor, introduced me to the technique. Brainspotting, a technique rooted in eye movement desensitization and reprocessing therapy (EMDR), posits that where someone looks affects their emotions. I was initially confused as to what it was and how it could work. Furthermore, where would it fit in a counseling session? The idea that we as counselors are not only working with another person, but also another person's brain, struck me.

The first time I was on the receiving end of brainspotting, I noticed the physical differences in myself as my eyes followed a pointer to different places. It was as if memories were neatly filed into various locations for my mind to recite when cued. The week of being trained in brainspotting, I noticed a sense of calm, and vivid dreams occurred. God had led me to such a powerful gift that had been hidden in plain sight.

I began using it in sessions to find that clients had various responses, from calmness to sensory experiences to effects outside of session. When in session, I felt like a wizard flicking a wand, watching how clients' symptoms and realizations would appear and disappear. Even in the early stages of brainspotting, I felt the freedom to be a showman as if performing magic tricks. My clients were mesmerized by the effects, and so was I.

Brainspotting also presented a kind of peace in its process and emphasis on not working too hard during a session, for both the counselor or client. To think that more results can be gained with far less work and less time seemed like a win all around.

Insight: Our Growth Parallels Our Clients

The truth is, as we grow, our clients grow. Sadly, I think if we remain complacent or stuck as therapists, our clients might, too. As much as some forms of counseling claim to be unbiased, the truth is that counseling by its very nature is biased. The story of the client is being processed through the lens of the counselor and the therapeutic relationship. Of course it's biased. What if you watched a movie with your best friend? Each of your experiences of the movie and viewing together brings more unique perspectives than if you each watched it separately.

Clients have told me they've seen me grow at various stages of my career, and it is reassuring to know that I have been seen by those I listen to and validate. When I started in the field and my eyes were opened to addiction, I started to take note of my own vices. In this way, much of my work was about identification of problems. Later, when I ran a wellness group for two years, I used the wellness lens to understand my habits and relationships as well as those of my clients. When I stood up for myself and needed to take better care of myself, I pushed the importance of self-care with clients, too. Then, when I realized I may have gone too far on the "self," I let my foot off the brake. Learning about brainspotting and seeing how it produced healing in me led me to introduce it into my own practice. As I read about purpose and listened to sermons on barriers to purpose, I began introducing more spiritual and existential topics with clients.

My Christian beliefs have become easier to integrate into my practice as well. When appropriate, faith has become a significant part of my work with clients. I started wearing my cross necklace to sessions and have never received a negative response to it. This was a big step for me in being open about my beliefs and faith. When appropriate, I share that I may be a biased source but that I don't have intentions to push religion or spirituality. Rather, I offer an invitation to explore the topic. I've navigated these topics better with believers and nonbelievers as my career and my faith have grown.

Sometimes I learn things from nonclinical sources that I bring to session. The Pixar movie *Inside Out* has been a helpful tool to characterize feelings or demonstrate the importance of recognizing and expressing our emotions. Songs, movies, sports, comedy, church sermons, and video games have made their way into sessions, sometimes as ways to express a point or create analogies. This is why I believe it's important for therapists to be well-rounded people. Counselors need to understand many areas of life to get a sense of their clients' perspectives. Additionally, being a well-rounded person gives therapists more to offer clients than blanket statements and cliché coping strategies. I imagine clients can tell if we're only portraying a therapist and hiding the person we really are.

I'm proud to say that as a counselor, I often respond, laugh, and share with clients in a similar way to how I interact with family and friends. I'm genuine. When I have my counselor hat on, I ask far more questions, and the relationship is predominately one-sided, focused on healing and guiding. My therapeutic relationships are very different in this way. However, my interactions and how I choose to present myself offers clients a glimpse of who I am. My qualities of being caring, patient, sensitive, kind, open-minded, and accepting gleam through no matter what role I'm in. My newer qualities of being confident, more outspoken, and more willing to stand up for myself also are starting to show.

Insight: Take Off the Counselor Hat

At a karaoke night, my friend, also a counselor, teased me to take off my counselor hat. We discussed how difficult it is to step away from this role, that it is embedded in our identities. I found myself over the course of that night offering psychoeducation, validation, and encouraging statements. I couldn't help but talk about these things. Outside the event, I overheard a woman telling her friend she could use a therapist. I almost cleverly handed her my business card, nearly failing to realize she was likely drunk and that this was not the moment to market my practice.

I've typically been a listener among my friends and, at times, the one they might text or seek for a listening ear. I see the world at times through a nonjudgmental lens that takes many angles of the story instead of jumping to conclusions. I analyze situations and often overthink decisions because I've considered many possibilities, viewpoints, and the ethical/moral side of the situation. At times this process is conscientious, well-informed, and understanding. Other times, it is obsessive, annoying, and unreasonably attached.

What excites and interests me also fits with the counselor identity. I feel honored when a friend shares their passion or tells me about a topic that is personal to them. I enjoy observing and understanding situations. The challenge of finding patterns in life is mentally stimulating, such as understanding what cards a person has in poker by their outward presentation or how much an athlete's career trajectory relates to their personality. I'm intrigued by the reasons businesses and teams succeed and fail. I'm fascinated by what brought a person or a couple to the point of conflict and at how simply the conflict can be resolved, whether in a healthy or unhealthy way. Humans are amazing. I guess that's why it's said that people don't become self-aware, great listeners, or caring because they're therapists. Instead, people who are insightful, enjoy listening, and care about others become therapists.

Chapter Fourteen
Conclusion

Three Things I Can Attest To

There are three things in life I can confidently stand behind that have changed and continue to change my life for the better — the love of God, the process of therapy, and genuine human connection. While a good portion of this book is dedicated to faith, simply put, God has been good to me. He's made ways for me when there seemed to be no clear path. He's offered clarity that surpassed my understanding. He's alleviated the pressure to figure out various issues, stressors, and confusion on my own. God has certainly given me more than I deserve, opened doors I couldn't have imagined would be there, and carried me when I had no strength to move forward.

Therapy, and by extension brainspotting, have brought understanding, insight, and calm to my clients and myself. God guided me to my therapists when I needed them. I had no idea that talking about my problems or looking at a tip of a pointer would help in my growth and healing from OCD and pain. I certainly didn't know that being helped would allow me to help others. Meanwhile, genuine human connection has reminded me of my purpose, importance, and value in this life. No one can live this life alone — we need others.

Year Six

My professional concerns were drastically different as I wrapped up my sixth year as a therapist than they were at previous points in my career. Issues entailed the most effective interventions for my clients and where I wanted to take my business, rather than how much paperwork I had to do, a key difference between agencies and private practice. I don't worry about what my boss might say because I am my boss. I don't allow drama to happen in my office, and I wear what I like. I feel I'm paid fairly, and my finances are in order. Work for me is exciting, liberating, and purposeful. It's something special that I happen to get paid to do.

I got to this place in six years. I didn't expect to be here. When I joined the field, I didn't even know who I might help. I stumbled and fell into some good situations and learned more than I could have imagined about the human experience and the impact a therapeutic relationship can have on a person's life. I learned more about how to manage my own mental health, which included my struggles with OCD; that people truly cared about me; and that God was with me the whole time, weaving a story of hope and healing. My hope is that this book gives you what you need to achieve your personal, spiritual, and professional dreams with insight, love, and, of course, your genuine self. I also hope that it brought understanding, validation, and encouragement to your personal struggles — you truly are not alone.

The End, at Least of This Book

Friends and clients, even my mom, began giving me the nickname of Mister Ross. I saw it as a sign of respect they would call me that, even when I preferred to go by my first name. I saw the similarities to Mister Rogers, one of my childhood heroes who I learned to appreciate even more as an adult. I took ownership of that nickname through naming my businesses Mister Ross Counseling LLC and Mister Ross Creations LLC. The title felt like it fit the professional yet personable persona I wanted to portray.

I don't think one day we wake up and simply become a new version of ourselves. Or that once we've become that person, there's no longer a process of becoming and adapting. For me, this is the beginning of my story, of how I became Mister Ross.

Epilogue

I'm thankful to each of you who took the time to read my book. It took me many hours of writing, editing, and procrastinating to put this together. It's easy to forget why you started writing a book in the first place, and this book has taken on new meaning with each draft. This book means so much more, as I've been inspired to extend my writing to short stories, poetry, and reflections. This is the tip of the iceberg for me, and I hope you will join me in reading more of my writing. I don't take for granted the gift of time we have, and I truly appreciate the time you took to learn about my experience.

I realized it's not easy to share one's experiences. I hesitated sharing mine with you. But it was time.

Acknowledgements

I would like to acknowledge many of the people who have had a profound impact on me personally and professionally, particularly those who supported me in the writing of this book.

First and foremost, I'd like to thank God for carrying me through some difficult times and for loving me unconditionally, consistently, and undeniably. You've given me more than I could have asked for, and I'm thankful for what You give me each day.

I thank my family for shaping the person I am and supporting me. To Mom and Dad, you've been there through the toughest and the best times. You've taught me about how to handle one's responsibilities and share with others. To my brother Paul, you've pushed me to be better and continue to be one of my best friends, a friendship that's different from any other. Thank you as well for your connections to a marketing team and an editor. To Grandma and Grandpa, you've shown you still watch over me. To my cat Gabby, you've become my most unlikely of best friends. You've helped me learn how to give and receive love unconditionally.

To my therapists, I wouldn't be here without you. You've helped me have a new perspective on life and gave me the validation and confidence to see the good in me that I didn't know was there. You've been among my biggest fans and gently encouraged me toward growth. To the late Dr. Robert Shaw, my life would be completely different without you. To Bill, you've been the mentor I hoped you would be and so much more. As you told me, if this book changes one life, it was worth it. Thank you as well for reading it and understanding my story on such a deep level.

To my many mentors, thank you for taking time to help me despite the multitude of responsibilities you had, both professional and personal. You took me under your wing and shared your passion with me, which in turn motivated me to share my passion with others. Kristy, you have been a guiding beacon as a supervisor, colleague, and friend.

To my friends, you make life that much more worthwhile. There are so many of you to thank, so simply put, thank you for being there, whether for a short time or a long time.

To those who guided me through their work, including the late Fred Rogers, Bob Ross, and Jim Henson. Thank you all for your work built on love for your craft and for others; I am inspired to help people as you all did. Irvin Yalom, your writing on therapy has been inspiring and insightful for me as I learned about this field. Jonah Hill and Dr. Phil Stutz, your documentary was evidence that people were looking for the kind of content I wanted to share.

To myself: You pushed through some tough times writing this book. The heartaches, headaches, anxiety, roadblocks, and procrastination. This was not an easy book to write, and you certainly could have spent or, worse, wasted your time doing other things. But you chose to write, and I believe you're better for it. Hopefully others are better for it, too. Whether this book sells 10 copies or is the next bestseller, God loves you more than you can imagine.

To my first editor, colleague, and friend, Megan, thank you for supporting and helping me build my story one typo, run-on sentence, or poorly worded phrase at a time.

To my good friend Sammie, thank you for reading this book and offering insightful feedback. You helped me feel validated and made me realize even more that resentment doesn't help us.

To Jeremy, thank you for encouraging my vision of content creation, listening to the first rendition of my audiobook, and offering inspiring and helpful guidance.

To those at the Christian Writers Sanctuary, especially Kim Wuertz and Deb Elliott, whose drive to shape writers has been inspirational.

To Caitlin, for the final edits to this book as I learned the author should not be the one to make the last edits.

To Brittany and Bethany at Market Share Consulting, you two were the missing pieces to make this happen from the logo to the cover to the site and marketing. Thank you for getting my dream off the ground.

And of course, to my clients. You've taught me about humility, mercy, gratitude, love, hopefulness, persistence, creativity, pain, and that mysterious, special part in all of us that keeps us going. Your trust in me brings out the best counselor in myself and, at times, the greatest spiritual connection I have with God. God has worked through our sessions to bring healing to you and lessons to me as I learned alongside you. I feel honored that you gave me the privilege to listen to your stories, sufferings, joys, and hopes.

About the author

Ross Capoccia, MA, LPC aka "Mister Ross" is a counselor, faculty member, and writer. In his free time, he enjoys line dancing, playing games, reading and performing poetry, watching the Denver Broncos, and spending time with his loved ones. He lives in a quiet neighborhood in Scranton, Pennsylvania with his cat, Gabby.

Enjoy Mister Ross' writing?

Follow Mister Ross at misterrosscreations.com for updates on publications, social media, and content.

Made in the USA
Middletown, DE
24 June 2024

56052994R00092